CREATING YOUR SALES TEAM

CREATING YOUR SALES TEAM

Belief Systems and Human Behavior in Sales:
Constructing a Culture

John M. Hanson

Preface

My writing of this book was inspired after 20 years of creating and managing my own sales team, and recognizing how much easier it would have been if someone had shown me a "how to" book on human behavior. I had to learn through "hard knocks" how to create a successful sales team. Through that, my inspiration came to share with others, these important discoveries that I had made. The past five years of managing a brokerage for other owners has helped me to come to conclusions that had been milling around in my mind. I've been able to watch these owners construct a culture, (and be a part of it), in going from 80 sales agents to over 300 in about four years.

I became a "book worm" of non-fiction, and most especially of books on human behavior, over the prior ten years. Coupled with my own experiences in management of sales people, I was bursting with the desire to share this knowledge with others who were struggling with their own sales team, or who were thinking about creating their own sales team.

In this book I share many of those "intangibles" that make the difference. Human behavior can be so unpredictable, but a manager can control her own thoughts and actions, the company's systems, and the company culture. The reader of my book, (who drinks it all in), will avoid subtle pitfalls, and preemptively create a fortress and systematic "machine of systems" that will glide through turmoil and changing markets while giving the manager a peace, joy, and confidence in the direction and course of the formation or reformation of the sales team. Enjoy the journey!

Contents

1

Re*In*Carnation

arnation, Washington, is a quiet rural town with fewer than two thousand residents. It is situated about twenty-five miles to the east of Seattle. The obscure rural community was thrust into the headlines on Christmas Eve of 2007 when something that happened there shocked the community, state, and much of the nation. It completely broke with what most of us would call normal. It involved the belief systems of two people that most of us will never understand. Let me give you some background.

In the early 1980s, Wayne and Judy Anderson had purchased a home in a rural private setting just outside of Carnation. Their three children were Mary, Scott, and Michele. The Andersons were a quiet, private family. Wayne worked as an engineer at Boeing in Seattle while Judy, in the early 1990s, started working as a postal carrier for the Carnation Post Office, a little two-window building. They were both well-liked, dutiful employees and were able to save enough money to eventually purchase an adjoining parcel of land next to their home. By the 2007 Christmas Eve tragedy, they had gated the property and placed a mobile home about two hundred yards from their house.

Their daughter Mary lived in nearby North Bend. Mary was very close to her mother and had even had a coffee shop business venture with her parents' good friend, Mark Bennett. At the time of the tragedy, she was out visiting other family members.

Just as the parents, Wayne and Judy, were friendly, likeable people, so too was their son, Scott. The thirty-two-year-old Scott lived with his wife, Erica (age thirty-two), and their two children, Olivia (age six) and Nathan (age three) in the town of Black Diamond, about a forty-five-minute drive from Carnation. They had a modest yellow house with a chain-link fence surrounding the backyard. Police visiting the home after the occurrence could see numerous toys in the backyard and Olivia's bicycle on the front porch. Neighbors described Scott as a "friendly guy" who "worked insane hours." He was a construction worker, and he painted cars as a sideline. His wife, Erica, was a stay-at-home mom. The two children were playful and happy, often seen waving to neighbors as they drove past their house. The family of four went to Carnation that Christmas Eve to celebrate with Scott's parents, Wayne and Judy Anderson.

Michele was the sister of Mary and Scott. "She had a different way of thinking," was what one relative later commented. She felt that her parents' love was not fairly meted out to the children and that she got the short end. Michele was unemployed at the time of the shocking incident. She had previously worked as a security guard and had once tried to start an auto-painting business called Pure Evil Customs. Her neighbors from her previous Fall City (near Carnation) mobile home park had described her as "volatile" and "angry" and said that she frequently commented on how she was financially struggling while her parents "had quite a lot." She had blacked out the windows of her Fall City home because of her fear that neighbors were spying and trying to break in. One relative said that there had been a long-standing fight between Michele and her parents and that she had been fighting with them since she was thirteen years old. She was angry because she didn't think her parents showed her enough love.

Michele had told a high school friend that she and her brother, Scott, had been abused by their father throughout their childhood. Michele's friend also said that she had been diagnosed with severe anxiety and was supposed to take medication and see a counselor but couldn't afford it. Her overall feelings seemed to be that she was tired of "everyone stepping on her." She felt unloved and disrespected. She felt unfairly treated, financially, by both her brother and by her parents.

But Michele was not acting alone on Christmas Eve of 2007. Five to six years before the horrible incident, Michele had met Joseph McEnroe through an online service. McEnroe was also twenty-nine years of age. He had been living in Arizona but moved up to the northwest to be with Michele. They had planned to get married. McEnroe's family in Arizona described the boy that they knew, growing up, as a nonviolent, quiet loner with a blood disorder and chronic nosebleeds. He read a lot and played video games as a boy. McEnroe quit high school to work at Burger King in his senior year. In his twenties, he spent much of his time online and playing Dungeons and Dragons. He and Michele lived together in the Fall City mobile home where they had blacked out all the windows. Their mobile home park neighbors said that the couple fought loudly and often and that McEnroe would "come and go all night long." One neighbor's opinion was that he was a "total loser." The couple's plan, on that 2007 Christmas Eve, was to confront the family with their perceived injustices. They were intent on killing everyone if "problems did not get resolved." By this time, they had left Fall City and had been living in the mobile home on Michele's parents' property right next door. Michele had been feeling pressured by her parents, Wayne and Judy, to pay rent.

Though living just two hundred yards away, Michele and her boyfriend, Joseph, drove to the house of Wayne and Judy Anderson around 4:00 p.m., Monday, December 24, 2007. The sixty-one-year-old Judy was in a back room wrapping gifts for her grandchildren. Michele and Joseph each had a handgun (a revolver and a nine-millimeter semiautomatic) as they entered the house. Michele fired the first shot at her father and missed. McEnroe then shot him in the head. From the back room, Judy heard the shots and came running out to the scene. McEnroe shot her once, and Judy fell to the floor, screaming. He then apologized and shot her in the head.

Unaware of what was happening at his parents' house, Scott packed up his family and began the drive from his Black Diamond home to spend Christmas Eve with his parents, who now lay dead on the floor. Knowing that her brother was on the way, Michele (and Joseph) hid the two bodies and cleaned up the blood with towels and rugs. When Scott, Erica, and their two children were in the house, Michele drew her gun. Scott immediately charged at her, and she fired two to four times, striking him at least once in the neck. Though she had been shot twice, Erica managed to climb over a couch to grab a cordless phone and call 911. Nothing was spoken, and the operator only heard yelling and noise during the ten-second call and thought that it was just a celebration. McEnroe had ripped the phone from Erica's hands, crushed it, and tossed the batteries to the floor. McEnroe had been the one designated to execute Erica and the two children, because Michele couldn't bear to do it herself. McEnroe allowed Erica to huddle with her children, six-year-old Olivia and three-year-old Nathan. He then shot and killed her. Next, he apologized to Olivia, put the gun up to her head, and shot her. Little Nathan had picked up one of the discarded batteries from the floor and looked up at McEnroe, who apologized, put the gun to the three year-old's head, and fired.

The murderous couple drove north toward Canada before turning around and heading south toward Oregon, only to turn around again and return to the now two-day-old crime scene, which swarmed with police. First feigning bewilderment, they eventually confessed, sharing the vivid details. Michele demanded the death penalty, wanting to take responsibility for her actions. Family members think that that would be an easy escape and instead want her to suffer in prison where she would have to live with the mental anguish of her gruesome crimes. McEnroe was sentenced to life in prison on May 13, 2015. Michele was also sentenced to life in prison in the fall of 2015.

For a family tragedy of this magnitude to have occurred is almost unfathomable. What was going on in the mind of Michele Anderson? Three different mental health specialists evaluated her, and each said that she was "sane and competent." How could her reality have been so different from the rest of her family's? What happened within her mind that led her to feel so victimized, so unloved, and so unfairly treated that she could rationalize her deeds? If she had been abused in her childhood, was that justification for her actions? Clearly, within her own reality, she had a strong sense of entitlement. There were certain things that her parents possessed that she felt entitled to. Clearly, within her own reality, her sense of fairness and justice was radically different from most of ours. Somehow, through her twenty-nine years of living, to that point, she had developed belief systems of entitlement and of fairness/justice that were very powerful. Her life's observations and subsequent interpretations of those observations framed a certain reality for her. How many internal conversations did she have to have in her conscious mind that were answered to herself according to her reality and then etched deep into her subconscious mind to form her belief systems? How much more deeply did those belief systems take root with a boyfriend to sympathize and perhaps emotionally enable her? How was Joseph McEnroe influenced by her impassioned pleas for love and understanding and her constant cries of injustice? Each time Michele verbally framed a story, according to her reality, for Joseph to hear, how much more convincing was that to both Joseph and to Michele's own subconscious mind?

Whether you are an employer, employee, manager, sales agent, or a customer or client, you have belief systems built within your subconscious mind from a lifetime of conscious, internal self-dialogues. Your interpretations and answers in those self-dialogues have formed your reality of *fairness/justice*, of *entitlement/arrogance*, of *accountability*, of *hard work*, of *discipline*, and of *success*. These six belief systems create a reality for a person that may not always lead to the type of crisis that Michele Anderson found herself wrapped into but certainly impacts how an employee will function, how a manager will interact with staff and clients, how clients will respond to products or services, and finally, how a company's culture will be formed.

Most books on management address mechanical issues within an office environment (e.g., who reports to whom, office policies, taxation, liability issues, and so on). Some even address subsurface issues like mission statements, discipline issues, tactical issues, and so on. The intent of this book is to delve into a deeper level of understanding, to address the cultural aspects of an office or company through an examination and an understanding of the individual belief systems of each person that ultimately form the company culture. It is the company culture that will drive the company. As the manager, it is your job to set that culture in place and maintain it.

It has been said that the definition of human behavior is "the mind driving the body in fulfillment of dominant thought." If business management is the utilization of other people to achieve company purposes, then understanding human behavior is, arguably, the most important skill that a manager has to master. With the definition of human behavior given here, knowing the dominant thoughts of each individual that you employ would be immeasurably more important than knowing how to complete an IRS form 1099 or how to fill out a floor schedule. A potentially employed or currently employed individual's dominant thoughts drive his or her behaviors, and it is the individual's belief systems that are the window to those dominant thoughts. If you, as a manager, want to predict the future actions of someone that you employ, simply find out what his or her belief systems are. Not so simple, right? Dominating thoughts on the conscious level of the human mind have been indelibly imprinted into the brain cells of the subconscious level of the mind. Also, a momentary conscious thought, if powerful and believable enough, is accepted and imprinted deep into the subconscious mind.

The conscious and the subconscious are not separate minds but faculties or levels of the same mind. They have different tasks. The task of the conscious level is to reason, judge, evaluate, and then accept or reject. When a thought is accepted on the conscious level, it moves into the subconscious level. The subconscious level of the mind doesn't judge or reason; it just does! It does whatever has already been judged and accepted at the conscious level of the mind. It (the thought) has been through the controllable strainer (conscious mind) and passed to the subconscious mind as what we call a *dominant thought*. All of those thoughts and ideas that are now embedded deeply into the fertile soil of the subconscious mind create the individual's belief systems. It is the collective finished product of thoughtfully worked-out reasonings of the human mind. The belief systems have formed the reality or *world view* of the individual. The subconscious mind will not decide right or wrong, good or bad. It will just carry out actions in alignment with already formed belief systems that were created by dominant thoughts. Only the conscious mind will accept or reject thoughts, concepts, and beliefs. Stephen Covey (*The 7 Habits of Highly Effective People*) wrote that between stimulus and response, there is choice. That is only true at the conscious level; it is not true at the subconscious level. The firmly established belief systems will defy the logic of many people and baffle the realities of many others, as in the case of Michele Anderson. But they are deeply rooted into an individual's subconscious mind, and the individual's natural defense mechanisms will defend those belief systems. You, the manager, will not change them through coercion, as hard as you might try. They must consciously desire to reprogram their own belief systems and their own behavior patterns.

To better understand this dynamic, let's examine a specific belief system. There are, of course, many that we could choose from, but let's start with the belief system of accountability. The natural defense mechanisms of the human psyche, at the subconscious level (also referred to as the *adaptive unconscious level*) will defend it and fight against accountability. They will resist the very thing that will help a sales agent, for example, to succeed. They will frantically form antiaccountability thoughts and create rationalizations that will quickly become emotions. Emotions, as you know, defy logic and in this case are extremely sour to the idea of having to report to someone, especially for a commissioned sales agent with a business background or other expertise. These wrong emotions are the enemy of accountability. The internal dialogues have taken place over a long period of time. "I'm tired of people telling me what to do." "I know twice as much as my boss." "Wait until I have my own business. I know how to run myself." These types of dialogues were taking place internally and also externally with the validation of caring friends or family. They became ensconced in the subconscious mind, and now the past internal and external dialogues come out in defense of that individual's ego.

In hiring employees and independent contractors (sales agents), the great manager must look for belief systems of disciplined thought, strong work ethic, and acceptance—embracing—of accountability. At the conscious level, we need to understand clearly, deeply, and rationally why accountability is so important to our success. As we do this and linger on the thoughts, it will begin to seep into the subconscious level of our mind. As it grows in our subconscious mind, the natural defense mechanisms that resist accountability start to ease up and allow the accountability to take place. It will only allow it, however, after the conscious mind has reasoned, thought it through to a logical conclusion, and accepted the concept. Listening to a motivational speaker or reading his or her message can help a lot in this process, but it isn't yet strong enough to fight the natural defense mechanism. The human mind has to have a consistent feeding of a rational, sound explanation for submitting to accountability. Regularly reading uplifting books or listening to audiobooks by people like Anthony Robbins, who logically and powerfully make a case for accountability, is a good way to do this. Reciting positive affirmations daily is another. It takes discipline to program the powerful subconscious mind so that it will allow the accountability. Neuroassociative conditioning is the best way to effect changes in behavior.

Anthony Robbins explains very well how neuroassociative conditioning works. Neurological messages are rapidly firing to and from the brain at an amazing and incomprehensible rate of speed. By associating those messages to either pain or intense pleasure, we condition our behavior. A consistent association, neurologically, with pain will deter that behavior. A consistent association, neurologically, with an intense pleasure will create actions that drive the behavior toward it. Accountability means that when a task is given and a consequence or a reward is applied and anticipated, the neuroassociatively conditioned mind of that employee will make it happen. The unconditioned mind will frantically seek out excuses and justifications for nonperformance.

Recently, a student from one of my management classes called me for some advice. She owns and manages a real estate brokerage in a small community of about twenty-five thousand residents. She shared with me that as a result of one of my classes, she had "cleaned house" and now had just eight sales agents, less than half of what she had just a couple of months earlier. (Gulp!) In the past, she had been afraid of losing those agents, and those sales agents knew it and controlled her every business decision. They were not being held accountable for their own actions. Subsequently their production was sagging, and their attitudes were horrible. She identified the problematic sales agents and fired them. Now, she continued, the remaining eight sales agents were focused, happy, and willing to be held accountable for production and activity. Like a magnet, new sales associates were coming to work at her office, and she was calling me to get my advice on the best way to welcome and start out all those new sales agents. (A reincarnation of sorts!) I've heard this same story many, many times. I have personally experienced it in my own real estate brokerage business several times.

The influence of fellow employees and sales agents who are negative and resist accountability will rot everything around it. It permeates the culture of the office, disempowers the manager, and spreads from agent to agent and employee to employee like a cancer. Cut those people out of your business *now*! Don't worry or fear the loss of time you have spent getting them and training them. Cut your losses now. Start fresh with a new, more carefully selected group, and begin the culture of accountability, a culture of discipline. Those who resist your logical persuasions to submit to accountability must be terminated from your employ, no matter how much potential they outwardly show to you.

This belief system of accountability is used here to illustrate how belief systems can affect your business. You can see in the previous illustration how a manager would be well served to be able to see into the window of each potential hire's reality or world view before hiring them. Their realities are displayed by their belief systems, and we will look at some specific questions to ask and some specific things to look for in potential employees further on in chapter 2 that will help identify belief systems that impact your business. You will see that I use a real estate brokerage business as a model throughout this book, but the same principles would apply to any business where salespeople are employed. The six specific belief systems that the manager should be trying to identify, both within him- or herself and within the sales agents and employees, are the following:

1.) *Accountability*—How much resistance will there be to being held accountable? How does a culture of accountability help the individual to perform to his or her maximum potential? How does a culture of accountability in the company empower the manager and maintain the emotional health of the company?

2.) *Hard work*—Do the many benefits of hard work ooze through the beings of your employees? Do they ooze through your being? What is the correlation between hard work and success? Do they (and you) logically understand that correlation?

3.) *Fairness and justice*—This vital issue encompasses both compensation issues and ethics. Victimhood, a condition of the mind, is addressed here, in chapter 6.

4.) *Arrogance and entitlement*—How do they see themselves in relation to other people? From what plane do they relate with clients or customers, fellow employees or sales agents, and management? How can belief systems of arrogance or of entitlement rot the culture of an office or of a company?

5.) *Discipline*—How does the cycle of discipline, from thought to action, work with them? Does the employee really seek discipline? Does the sales agent? Does the client? Do you, the manager?

6.) *Success*—What makes success? Is it natural talent? Is it hard work? Is it luck? Is it circumstance and positioning? How does a potential employee's belief in the manner that success is accomplished affect how he or she works and how he or she interacts with others in your office or company?

There are many more belief systems that people have formed that will impact various aspects of their lives, but these six are the most important in business. We will examine each one, how it affects the manager, the employee or sales agent, and the client or customer. The established belief systems of a nation, a community, or an individual might very well be the sales agent's, marketer's, client's, or manager's best friend or their greatest enemy. Whether a particular belief system is a friend or an enemy depends on the manager's approach to that person or to the manager's business culture. You cannot convince or soften the opinion of someone who is already deeply entrenched in his or her own belief systems. Just try to convince a third-generation Baptist of the message of Mormonism or of Kingdom Hall. Try to change the mind of a government-dependent US citizen from one of the coasts of the merits of low taxes and free enterprise, or try to change the mind of a small business owner of the merits of high taxes and government mandates. The belief system of a person, once established, defends itself. It has already become part of the individual's identity.

Throughout a person's life, others impose their own realities or world views upon him or her, and he or she either resists with resolve or else caves in to someone else's will. What he or she doesn't know is that each person trying to hook his or her attention is just trying to justify his or her own reality and belief system. In *this person's* reality, which I will now call a story, *he or she* is the main character. Each person is the main character of his or her own story. Everyone else is a secondary character who is used to fill the main character's story. A parent, for example, will often be happy or mad at his or her child, based upon how well the child is playing his or her secondary role in the father's or mother's story.

When someone tries to impose his or her will upon you to make you the secondary character in his or her story (that he or she wants you to be), you naturally rebel. Sometimes it becomes frustrating and confusing for others when they would like you to play a secondary role in their story, and it is different from the main character role that you currently play in your own story. But it's your story! Know who really cares about *you* and who might be using you as a secondary character in their own story. Be yourself and let other people be themselves. If they want to be a primary or secondary character in their own story, that's their reality. That's their story.

It doesn't have to be true to you—just to them. You are only responsible for what you feel and believe. Others are responsible for their own stories. Don't take their realities or stories personally. It's not necessarily the truth; it's only true to them. Embrace your own reality and business model as your truth and wave that banner high to recruit staff and sales agents with a similar reality. This is the most important step in the creation of a sales team or in a reincarnation of your team.

The leader of a team within a real estate office seems to face this on a constant basis with recruiting a showing agent, buyer's agent, or listing agent. Much time and training is invested only to have that agent leave with the perception that there is more money or an easier way somewhere else. The biggest part of that selection process needs to be an analysis of the loyalty of the agent and his or her recognition of the benefits. As leaders, it is our responsibility to frame the benefits for them and help them recognize and appreciate them. Instead of trying to sell those benefits to someone incapable of loyalty and who is always looking for the bigger, better deal, find individuals with like minds and belief systems.

The human psyche, early on in its life, seeks out stability—solid ground on which to stand, so to speak. It seeks out a framework for the confusing world around it and how it fits into that world. Once a belief system is formed, the human mind must defend that belief or the once firm earth shakes under its feet. The mind asks and answers billions of questions faster than the speed of light. These beliefs become so powerful because they are deeply embedded in the subconscious mind. The subconscious mind is always very hard at work, even while we are sleeping. It confirms and reconfirms, reinforces and cements once consciously formed beliefs deeply into the being of the individual. That person's circle of friends and associates confirms those subconsciously held beliefs on a daily basis. To accept a different belief would not only shake the framework of the person's psyche; it could also shake their family and social structure as well. To allow even a window of doubt into a staunch belief system shakes a person to the very core. The belief system is powerful! Try to sell sliced bread to a generation of Americans who sliced their own. This convenience took decades and clever marketing to catch on. Try selling to the American Medical Association the idea that centuries of theories about ulcers were wrong and that it's the *Helicobacter pylori* bacteria that causes ulcers, not spicy food or stress. It took twenty years and a Nobel Peace Prize for the old belief system to change from so many years of assumption. Belief systems are tightly woven into the very fabric of the individual, and the resistance and stubbornness to change are so strong that to expect a change in an employee's behavior is like asking my dog not to bark at the neighbor's dogs. It is possible but highly improbable. It is much more effective to identify the relationship between the aforementioned six belief systems and the behaviors that you can expect within the office as a result. Only then can you, the manager, begin asking the right questions in the selection process and begin implementing systems that will create a culture that is conducive to success. Build or rebuild (reincarnation) a company culture that flows with the right people and the right office systems, all in alignment with the right belief systems for your business model.

2

White Oleander
(Hiring and Staffing Issues)

Whether it's an office, a family, a church, or whatever group of people, one of the most devastating things to that culture or environment is what I call a "white oleander." Literally, white oleander is a shrub with fruit that blossoms a beautiful, pure white color. The white oleander is often sweet scented. It's a pretty attractive package on the outside, but it is also one of the most poisonous plants known to man. My point here is that within an office culture, it is very common for a certain individual to emerge with a happy, helpful, and caring persona that naturally elicits the trust and confidence of coworkers or fellow sales agents in the office. Subtly, that individual begins to poison the environment. He or she is probably unaware of what he or she is doing on a conscious level, but the belief systems of the subconscious mind are deviously at work.

In wars involving the United States, the American prisoner of war has shown strong resistance to torture and also to the enticement of freedom in exchange for information. So, in the Korean War, the Chinese Communists introduced a new way of getting the American POWs to talk. It was to spend long hours in calm conversation, trying to get the American POW to concede small points of philosophy like, "The United States isn't perfect" or "Communist countries have 0 percent unemployment." Once they had gotten them to concede these small points, they could expand and widen the conversation, ever so gradually, until the soldier would at least feel sympathy for the communist cause or at best defect to their side. It is a technique that is similar to the one used by the "white oleanders" of the office.

The trust is built first. The white oleander's conversations begin with pleasant, innocent-sounding comments like, "She's a nice manager, but did you know that…" or "I love this company, but don't you think that with all of these sales agents' commission splits going into it, it could at least afford to buy us a…" The poison to the office environment is a slow drip, pulling away the authority of the manager. The white oleander doesn't do this on a conscious level. These people see themselves as dutiful and loyal. It is on the subconscious level that these behaviors are unleashed. Their realities or belief systems are internally colluding to bring about a result that they feel will position them or empower them within the office. In a sales office, such as real estate, it is particularly prevalent because there isn't normally an advancement hierarchy. Their belief system of being promoted has been ingrained in them since grade school, so where no such option exists, their subconscious mind creates one.

The culture and cohesiveness of the office is quietly being torn apart like a thread being pulled out of a piece of fabric. It will culminate in either the collapse of the office or the manager firing that sales agent. If the firing takes place too late, many other sales agents will follow the white oleander out the door and into his or her newfound office. If he or she is not recognized and terminated from your employ quickly, the white oleander's cuts and digs at the office, at real estate sales as a viable profession, and at clients (with comments like "Buyers are liars" and so on) will fester and grow like a cancer.

My personal business background was managing a real estate brokerage for more than twenty-five years. In a large real estate brokerage, you have a handful of employees and a lot of salespeople who are independent contractors. Among those sales agents, there will emerge the subtle, quiet, attractive white oleanders and the overt, more easily recognizable prima donnas. Look at free agency in professional sports. Free agency causes team management fits once each year when some of the contracts end. Imagine an arena like real estate brokerage where every salesperson is a

free agent every single day! They could shop themselves daily to competing firms to *bid* on their affiliation. Those competing firms are recruiting
your salespeople on a constant basis! The inducements are insane! It is
insanity! Typically, a manager will bend over backward to keep and attract
salespeople, often at the cost of running in the red financially, with spending exceeding income in order to please everybody. I had the opportunity
to acquire a few of these offices, a particular one that was losing $6,000
each month and another that was losing $9,000 each month. (Did I just
say, "I had the opportunity…"?). That's a lot of loss for a small business.
In both cases, the manager was being driven by his or her subconscious
fear—the fear of having sales agents recruited away by competitors. Those
managers were nice people with a belief system saying, "If I spend, they
will come," and that existing agents will not leave. Wrong! The result was
financial collapse, after years of negative cash flow. Each salesperson had
his or her own special itch to be scratched, and the manager would scratch
it even though he or she knew that it wouldn't fit in the budget. Why did
those managers do it? One of those two managers was a former career state
government manager whose belief system was that certain things were necessities and that somehow the money would magically appear. (This false
and dangerous belief system says that you have to spend money to make
money.) Think of governors, US presidents, senators, or congresspeople
who have to please their constituents to get elected or reelected. They
promise everything to everyone, and when the budget reality hits, they
have to either filch on their promise to someone or tax the people more. To
justify the tax, they use age-old excuses like, "We can't starve the children"
(children always melt hearts), or "We can't leave the elderly out in the cold
street" (ditto to the heart melting), or "We'll have to cut school programs"
(such as sports—that always hits home), and so on. All the politicians really have to do is stay within the budget and cut spending on the lowest
priorities. But if they do, they will lose that segment of their voter base.
And so it is with managing the budget in your business. You can't make
everyone happy and stay solvent. The answer is accountability, once more.
One of the six critical belief systems to understand and utilize to your

advantage is accountability with follow-through on consequences for poor performance or for inaction. Good salespeople, with a healthy set of belief systems, respect that kind of management. Those who have a belief system of loyalty toward good management will not be lured away by a competitor. (That last statement is a fact, and yet it clashes with the belief system of many managers.)

It takes incredible courage for a manager to hold firm on the budget and to allow competitors to lose their own money on frivolously overpaying sales agents or overspending to please them. A great manager can help commissioned salespeople make more money by holding them accountable than they would make from a higher commission split or other business perks. How could that be? It's all about the belief system! We will see exactly how this works in chapter 4, entitled "Accountability."

The belief systems of discipline and accountability throughout the company are what create a company culture. It is not possible for a manager to alter or delve into the belief system of each individual within the company, so the great manager must implement systems within the office that all employees or sales associates can align themselves to. Those systems and processes will be explained in each subsequent chapter. Those office systems and processes are the second of three things that a manager must do to start or restructure a company culture. The other two things are to get the right people with their accompanying belief systems on board and then to exercise discipline in the implementation of the office systems and processes. The order of those three things is of utmost importance. The order is the following:

1.) Hire the right people with the right belief systems that will align with your desired company culture.
2.) Develop and implement systems and processes that employees and sales agents can align themselves with and that will bring out their maximum potential.
3.) Exercise discipline in the performance of those systems and the daily, continual improvement of each system.

The reason that the order is so important is that when you have the right people in place, those people will develop the systems and processes. It is a distinction that is conducive to the culture of the company. If you, the manager, set the systems and processes and give those orders, the eventual results of those systems hinges upon your prior insights alone. By engaging the right people in that process, (as Jim Collins points out in *Good to Great*), you are borrowing upon the genius of people with expertise in those specific areas. The wrong people with the wrong belief systems will steer your office culture askew. So, learn to recognize the white oleanders (and anyone else who doesn't have your best interests at heart), and do not hire them. If you already have them in your employ, they must be terminated immediately. These are tough calls to make.

In the selection and interview process, how can you know whether or not the potential employee or sales agent will turn out to be a white oleander or a prima donna or have other belief systems that will affect the office culture that you are trying to achieve? Ori and Rom Brafman, in their book *Sway*, examine the hiring dilemma with the help of Professor Allen Huffcut, who studied job-interview diagnostic moments for twenty years.

> The standard job interview questions are familiar to all of us. But they make Huffcut cringe. During our conversation with him, he shared a list of the top ten most commonly asked questions during an interview…
> 1.) Why should I hire you?
> 2.) What do you see yourself doing five years from now?
> 3.) What do you consider to be your greatest strengths and weaknesses?
> 4.) How would you describe yourself?
> 5.) What college subject did you like the best and the least?
> 6.) What do you know about our company?
> 7.) Why did you decide to seek a job with our company?
> 8.) Why did you leave your last job?
> 9.) What do you want to earn five years from now?

10.) What do you really want to do in life?

Take question number three, about the candidate's greatest strengths and weaknesses. "What do you really gain by asking that?" Huffcut points out, "who's going to tell you their true weaknesses? I'm not going to say, "well, you know, sometimes I stay out late at night drinking and I'm late for work…" They're going to say something that sounds good but doesn't really portray a weakness: "Sometimes I try to do things too well" or "Sometimes I take my work too seriously."

The only one of the ten questions that Huffcut considers to be a viable question is number six: What do you know about our company? The other nine questions are too easy to spin. With respect, I disagree with that analysis and this is why.

To create and maintain the office culture that you desire, the most important element of the interview is not the questions that you ask; it is that you maintain control throughout the interview. There is a natural power struggle for that control that goes on in the interview session. The salesperson or independent contractor, for example, may believe that he or she is interviewing the manager to see if the brokerage will be deserving of his or her affiliation. If the manager, in the interview, fields the sales agent's questions, trying to sell the sales agent on the company, then control is in the sales agent's hands. That control will continue during the entire period of his or her employment. If, however, during the interview, the manager wrests control from the sales agent and puts the sales agent in a position of fielding questions and selling him- or herself to the manager, then the period of employment has a chance of succeeding. The control of the interview begins right away. So you (the manager) need to take charge immediately by saying something like, "Let's just both relax and feel comfortable asking a few questions of each other and getting to know one another. If it's OK with you, I'll start first by asking you some questions." That type of approach puts control in your hands and respectfully puts the sales agent in a docile position. If he or she did come in thinking that he or she was going to be interviewing you, that notion will be quickly dispelled. When he or she realizes what is happening, he or she will also respect you and regard you much more highly. This is the foundation that you want for a true working relationship!

The questions that you ask of the interviewees aren't as important as your interpretations of the answers given back to you, as long as the questions are open-ended, not yes-and-no-type questions. For example, if you ask, "What did you like the best about your last job?" their responses can reveal a lot about their belief systems, if you are carefully observing. You can't be thinking about your next question or wondering how *you* are coming across to *them*. Have a written list of preselected questions that you can ask. And have a notepad so that you can write down your impressions. Simply having the notepad and being busily engaged in writing while they speak will be impressive to them and is part of the control issue in the interview session. If their response to the question about their last job is, "Nothing! I couldn't wait to leave. It was a joke. They were so lame over there." Well, you just got a huge look into the window of their belief systems. You can now better understand who they are as a person and how they will interact in your work environment. They couldn't think of one thing that they liked about their last job? Really? Come on! Here, you must resist the temptation to interject with your own two cents and instead prod them gently with a follow-up question like, "What did they do over there that made them so 'lame'?" Now the window opens even wider. The same interviewing skill demonstrated here can work with several of those previously mentioned ten questions. As long as the questions that you ask are open-ended, you are establishing control and you are observing the window into their belief systems.

My worst hire ever occurred long before I learned these skills. A seasoned real estate agent phoned me to tell me that he was leaving his current office affiliation and that he wanted to see if my office might work out for him. While still on the phone with him, I asked him if he would mind my calling his current manager, and he told me that that would be fine. So, prior to his arrival at my office, I telephoned his manager. I asked the manager if he knew that the sales agent (whom I will call Mike) was leaving his employ, and he said, "Yes, I asked him to leave!" I was a bit startled by that because my impression from Mike was that he was quitting, not being let go. I asked the manager, "Why?" and he said that Mike and some fellow agents at his office just didn't get along very well. I asked if the agent's production was good, and he told me that it was good. The whole conversation with that manager seemed odd. There were too many pauses and awkward silences. There was a strange tone to the conversation. I was suspicious to say the least.

When the agent, Mike, arrived at my office, I was prepared to both hire him and get to the bottom of the oddness in my conversation with his prior manager. Mike had a kind of "good old boy" way of talking (slow and countryish) and liked to talk about his high production, which I later discovered was overinflated by at least four times. He also brought up specific clients and listings that he was currently working on and stated commission amounts in a slow, emphasized manner. Then he would say something like, "I don't know if that interests you at all, but I get kind of excited about all that money."

I asked him (and this is tongue-in-cheek) dazzling, brilliant questions like, "How did you get along with other people in your previous office?" or "Are you honest in your dealings with your clients?" Are you surprised that he answered just how I wanted him to, since I wanted to hire him? Oh… my…gosh! I couldn't have been worse, but in my own mind, I thought that I was really getting to the root of things.

I did hire Mike, and it was an enormous mistake, culminating in my having to let him go after a year and a half of destruction. Mike's way with customers and clients had resulted in frequent complaints to me. The complaints were usually emotionally charged, but no one could ever pinpoint exactly what it was that he did wrong. It was, in retrospect, just his way of exaggerating things, withholding information, and then soft-selling his agenda in a sly, sneaky manner. Sound familiar? It should. That's exactly how Mike talked to me in my first interview with him. I spent several years after his departure in litigation that resulted from his actions. Yet, the window into who he was and what his belief systems were was wide open for me to look into in that initial interview. Let me try to explain my poor decision by going back to Ori and Rom Brafman's book *Sway* and Malcolm Gladwell's book *Blink*. In *Sway*, the Brafmans write,

> Each day we are bombarded with so much information that if we had no way to filter it, we'd be unable to function. Psychologist Franz Epting, an expert in understanding how people construct meaning in their experiences explained, "We use diagnostic labels to organize and simplify. But any classification that you come up with," cautioned Epting, "has got to work by ignoring a lot of other things—with the hope that the things you are ignoring don't make a difference. And that's where the rub is. Once you get a label in mind, you don't notice things that don't fit within the categories that do make a difference."
>
> What Epting is saying is that all of us put on diagnostic glasses when we encounter new people…but we pay a price for these shortcuts, explained Epting: "The baggage that comes with labeling is the notion of the blinders, really. It prevents you from seeing what's clearly before your face…" When you think about it, the standard job interview is a lot like a first date. As Huffcut explained, "You don't have a clear format to follow and you just let the interview go as it will." Sitting across from a candidate, managers try to form an impression: Does the candidate share my interests? How's the chemistry between us? Is there a connection? Your typical unstructured interview—the common "first-date" method—just doesn't do well. We have a long history of research confirming that.
>
> Just how "not well" is surprising. When researchers conducted a meta-analysis—a broad study incorporating data from every scientific work ever conducted in the field—they found that

there's only a small correlation between first-date (unstructured) job interviews and job performance. The marks managers give job candidates have very little to do with how well those candidates actually perform on the job.

Speed dating is a modern way that people can sit around a room, take turns going around talking with each person, and select who they might be interested in knowing further. It saves people a lot of time, when they know how important that first impression really is to them. In *Blink*, Malcolm Gladwell writes,

> Suppose I were to alter the rules of speed-dating just slightly. What if I…made everyone explain their choices? We know, of course, that that can't be done: The machinery of our unconscious thinking is forever hidden. But what if I threw caution to the winds and forced people to explain their first impressions and snap judgments anyway? That is what two professors from Columbia University, Sheena Iyengar and Raymond Fisman, have done, and they have discovered that if you make people explain themselves, something very strange and troubling happens…Iyengar is a psychologist. Fisman is an economist. The only reason that they get involved in speed-dating is that they once had an argument at a party about the relative merits of arranged marriages and love marriages…The two professors run their speed dating nights…across from the Columbia campus. They are identical to standard New York speed-dating evenings, with one exception. Their participants don't just date and then check the yes or no box. On four occasions—before the speed-dating starts, after the evening ends, a month later, and then six months after the speed-dating evening—they have to fill out a short questionnaire that asks them to rate what they are looking for in a potential partner on a scale of 1 to 10. The categories are attractiveness, shared interests, funny/sense of humor, sincerity, intelligence,

and ambition. In addition, at the end of every "date," they rate the person they've just met, based on the same categories. By the end of their evenings, then, Fisman and Iyengar have an incredibly detailed picture of exactly what everyone says they were feeling during the dating process. And it's when you look at that picture that the strangeness starts…For example, if Mary said at the start of the evening that she wanted someone intelligent and sincere, that in no way means she'll be attracted only to intelligent and sincere men. It's just as likely that John, whom she likes more than anyone else, could turn out to be attractive and funny but not particularly sincere or smart at all. Second, if all the men Mary ends up liking during the speed-dating are more attractive and funny than they are smart and sincere, on the next day, when she's asked to describe her perfect man, Mary will say that she likes attractive and funny men. But that's just the next day. If you ask her again a month later, she'll be back to saying that she wants intelligent and sincere…Mary has an idea about what she wants in a man, and that idea isn't wrong. It's just incomplete. The description that she starts with is her conscious ideal: what she believes she wants when she sits down and thinks about it. But what she cannot be as certain about are the criteria she uses to form her preferences in that first instant of meeting someone face-to-face. That information is behind the locked door.

With those insights into the unpredictability of first-meeting hiring decisions, we come to a better understanding of the importance of having preselected, written questions in your hand while conducting interviews and of how writing down your observations while they answer helps you to stay on track with the belief system profile of the employee or sales agent that you are desirous of employing. Going back now, to my poor hiring decision of Mike, I should have recognized my own circumstances of that moment, which were that I was frustrated with low office production and wanted a sales agent with experience and production. I had blinders on with regard to Mike's belief systems and how his hiring would affect the culture of the office. I should have asked an open-ended question of him and paid attention to his verbal and nonverbal responses. Mike was the antithesis of the belief systems that I wanted to have and foster in my company, and hiring him set me back a couple of years, not to mention all the extra stress from doing damage control and litigation. It's as if I invited it into my doors.

Here is a list of some open-ended questions that I came up with that I think can help open the windows into the belief systems of employee candidates, if you observe their responses closely:

1.) If I were to ask the person who knows you the best to describe you to me in twenty words or less, what would that person say about you?
2.) What did you like the best about your last place of employment and why?
3.) What bothered you the most about your last place of employment and why?
4.) What makes you happy?
5.) By definition, what does success mean to you?
6.) What makes you feel fulfilled in life?
7.) Whom do you greatly admire and why?
8.) What is the relevance of your formal education to this job?
9.) If, through emergency, you had to be in isolation for an extended period of time and you had just a moment to decide on which three personal belongings to take with you, which three would you bring and why?
10.) What do you like to do when you have free time and why?

I believe that if you ask any of these types of questions and really closely observe their responses, you will see that window open up and the candidates will reveal themselves. It could be as simple as them muttering to themselves as they try to process the question or as deep as their psychological analysis. But what I know is that what they say and how they say it will be the same way they interact with clients and others in your office. Don't have blinders on during the interview!

Whether it is a white oleander who is poisoning the culture of your office or a blatant prima donna (a good producer with an overinflated sense of self who loves to boisterously challenge your authority.), this person must be rooted out very quickly, no matter what the perceived financial blow. The office that was losing $9,000 a month, which I mentioned earlier in this chapter, had eight prima donnas who had been controlling that manager's overspending actions for years! If they wanted something (like a helium machine to blow up balloons), they would tell him to get it or else they might have to go work from a competitor's office where they could get it. Out of fear of losing sales agents to the competition, that manager would kowtow to their every whim. He couldn't stand the thought of having his agents go elsewhere, and they knew it.

This brings us to a salient point that must be interjected here, because of the bravado I'm speaking with, of firing prima donnas and white oleanders. They have belief systems that have developed into these monsters. But they themselves are fellow human beings, deserving of dignity and kindness and a hope for shifting their belief systems. The analogy I want to use here is one that I discovered while watering my lawn one evening.

It was a particularly hot summer, and lawns were dying all over town. I was determined to keep mine looking good but had to be conservative with the water for both the financial and the environmental aspects. I chose to hand-water for more effectiveness and accuracy. Having only so much time, I had to continually face the decision of whether to water grass that was already a rich, healthy green or to use the water and my time to water the brown, seemingly dead portions of the lawn. I realized that if I put water and time into the dead or dying grass, I would be depleting water and time that would keep the thriving, healthy grass in that verdant condition. I would be risking losing the strength and vigor of the great to sacrifice for the dead or dying. It came to be my summer conundrum. It was my conundrum for both the grass and for its management comparison. Do we, as managers, spend time and resources on "dead and dying" sales agents or on the "healthy," hardworking agents? How much damage would it cause to the office culture and how many healthy, green sales agents do we sacrifice while trying to change dead and dying agents' belief systems?

For my lawn, I chose to focus most of my water and time on the healthy, green grass but still keep the dead and dying grass moist. It worked well. The brown grass came around a bit, and the green got really green! The good sales agents resent the time and energy that you spend on bad, failing agents, and the attitudes of the bad, failing agents poison the atmosphere for everyone. My conclusion to the office management conundrum is that you cannot afford to act on your natural compassion and desires to help everybody. The risk is too great to the sales agents in the company with a really low possibility of ever changing someone's belief systems.

In 2015, the Seattle Seahawks football team had a great defensive player named Kam Chancellor who had been an integral part of two straight trips to the Super Bowl. With three more years to go in his current contract, Kam decided to sit out until the team renegotiated his contract. The Seahawks were put in a tough spot, especially after starting the season off with a 0–2 start. They didn't budge and before their third game of the season, Kam showed up at practice to join his team…without a new contract. Had the Seahawks given in and reworked the contract, who would be next? And what kind of problems would capitulating to Kam's demands have caused to the team as a whole? They forced Kam to make a decision: his personal desires or the team and its best interests.

Also, because you are dealing with a white oleander or a prima donna, the chances of collateral damage upon terminating them from your employ are huge. The white oleander will work quietly, seductively, and manipulatively behind the scenes trying to recruit as many agents from your office to his or her new office with him or her, when he or she leaves. The prima donna is more overt but just as dangerous to your company. This person should not just be quietly let go. Without creating liability for your company by exposing details of the termination, you must let the rest of the office know that *you* terminated *him or her*. The story these people will spin to their new managers would be shocking to you (if you didn't understand belief systems), and the tales that they will spin to other sales agents at their new office and at your offices will be glaringly different from actual events, to say the least. To prepare for their false assertions, you need to make a statement to the people in your office like, "It is my duty as the manager to make sure that the working environment for you is always conducive to success. Tom Jones was terminated from our office yesterday in an effort to maintain the financial health and attitude of the office." No more needs to be said. When you are building a culture within the office, the rest of the sales agents (those who mesh with your culture) will understand.

I did feel it necessary, on one occasion, to do a dramatic announcement. After mulling the decision over for weeks, I fired ten sales agents from my two offices. At least three of them were very high producers but were problematic prima donnas. Since they were, unbeknownst to me, being recruited by a competitor up the street, they all went to that same office. I had hoped it would soar under the radar and that I wouldn't have to say anything. But immediately I heard the talk in my offices about how there was a mass exodus from my office to that specific competitor. I held my normal meeting that week at a local restaurant that had an aquarium with tropical fish that would be situated right behind me. I told them that the restaurant owner had a duty to keep those tropical fish fed and healthy and that if one of the fish were to die, it would float to the top and begin to rot. "One of the unpleasant tasks of the owner would be to quickly dip it out of the aquarium and flush it down the toilet. That way, it keeps the environment unspoiled for the healthy fish. In like manner, I have a duty to keep the environment of the offices unspoiled by rotting agents who are either a financial burden or an attitude problem. I recently had to dip ten sales agents out of our company aquarium and flush them down the toilet in order to keep the environment healthy for all of you. Ironically, the plumbing all seems to flow to the same office where you will currently find those who were fired from our company." Yes, I know that it could have ruffled feathers and possibly escalated even further. But I knew that it needed to be addressed or the spin from those departed sales agents would have caused great damage to my company. The terminations needed to happen, and I needed to be politically expedient in the aftermath.

It's all part of creating and maintaining a desirable culture that will align itself with the belief systems of the most desirable sales agents and staff. Recognition of white oleanders and prima donnas, with their immediate terminations from your employ, will form the culture that is necessary for the emotional health of your office. As Jim Collins puts it in *Good to Great*, "Get the right people on the bus and get the wrong people off the bus." That, as a reminder from earlier, is the first step to forming the office culture that you desire. It is the first step because with the right people in place, both sales agents and salaried staff, they will develop the proper systems for your office that will dovetail with your belief systems of accountability (which we will discuss in detail in chapter 4). The third and final step toward building the office culture that you desire is to exercise discipline in adherence to those systems, in working out the kinks, and in continuously improving each system (which we will discuss in detail in chapter 8, "Discipline").

After reading The Starbucks Experience and then a biography of the great UCLA basketball coach, John Wooden, I was struck by the fact that the five essential building blocks for a successful person within their systems were the same and were the same five that I had learned to look for in prospective sales agents, who should be the following: 1) welcoming and friendly; 2) genuine, sincere, and loyal; 3) respectful, considerate, and cooperative; 4) knowledgeable and industrious; and 5) engaging and energetic. When you talk to someone, you can see these things in their expressions, in their walk and movements, in the words they use, and in their voice.

As I began to build my own office in the mid-1980s, I needed to hire a staff person who could handle my trust account and my general account and help me support the sales agents as I began to acquire them. I used temp agencies or employment agencies to interview potential candidates. I was looking for someone with office skills like word processing, bookkeeping, and computer expertise. I couldn't pay very much, but I still had a lot of candidates that I got to interview. I would choose the candidate with the most skill and education. I found myself having to hire someone new for that position about every six months, because the people would find higher paying jobs, that or they would be a poison to the culture of my office and have to be let go. After about three years of this pattern, I recognized what I was doing and changed the pattern. I found a personal acquaintance who had never been employed but who I knew had the right belief systems. She had dedicated her life to raising children and doing volunteer work in the community. She believed in honesty, hard work, accountability, and discipline and felt no entitlements. Instead, she felt gratitude and flattery that I would even want to hire her, but most important, she cared very much about me and my family. She wanted to see my business succeed as badly as I wanted it to succeed. She was the perfect hire, inventing and building systems, positively influencing the sales agents, and staying with me for sixteen years. Toward the end, I was able to pay her well, give her Christmas bonuses, and send her and her husband on an Alaska cruise. She was not technologically skilled, educated in management, or exceptionally quick with her tasks. But she had good belief systems and she was an enormous blessing in my life.

3

Hie to Kolob!
(Identifying Your Core)

There are real estate firms that are 100 percent desk-fee offices, license-holding or fee-per-transaction offices, traditional commission-split offices, profit-sharing offices, franchises, independents, large offices, small offices, and many combinations or variations on any of the aforementioned. The business model that a manager uses is important—but only to that manager. Clients, customers, and sales agents have their own perceptions of what is the best. They will be drawn to it based on their own belief systems. If that were not true, everyone would stay at Motel 6, not the Westin, drive a Subaru, not a BMW, shop at Sears, not at Nordstrom—you get the idea. There isn't any *one* that's better than the other; they're just different and as such, appeal to different people at different times and in different situations.

Recently, I watched a particular comedian's stage routine. Part of his act was to use his funny voice and say (in paraphrase), "Oh, so we're both worshipers of Jesus Christ and embrace him as our Lord and Savior, trying to live the tenets of peace, love, and forgiveness. But you think of Jesus slightly different than I do...*so you must die!*" I laughed when I heard it because of my observations over the years of Christian churches; selecting two in particular, both worship Jesus Christ, but one believes that the Father and the Son are one and the same being who utilizes different titles and dwells in heaven, also known as paradise. The other Christian church believes that the Father and the Son are two separate and distinct personages who are so unified in purpose that they are as one, and dwell in heaven, also known as Kolob (Hence their church hymn "Hie to Kolob"). Members of the two different churches accuse the others of not being "true Christians" and cannot understand their stupidity or lack of understanding of the scriptures! They each have a belief system that has helped them to plant their feet firmly and to feel purpose and understanding of their existence. They have each formed their own realities, and if they were to read this, then they would say emphatically, "My belief *is* reality. It's not just *my* reality!" They each *know* that they are correct and the other group is sadly misguided. They will each defend, justify, and rationalize their point to the bitter end. Why?

Through a child's experiences, exposure to various stimuli, and desire to find acceptance, social structure, and an identity, he or she grows up attaching him- or herself to a belief. The defense mechanisms of the human psyche come out with all claws bared when challenged by an opposing belief that could possibly shake the firm ground on which it stands and threaten its social framework. Without even a conscious effort, the subconscious mind is already armed and ready to fight.

Hie to Kolob! The phrase literally means, "Hurry to the place where God dwells," according to one particular belief. To them, the name *Kolob* is just a name. The names that that religion usually uses are *heaven*, *paradise*, and so on. *Kolob* is rarely used. *Hie* is an old-fashioned word that means "hurry" or "speed up." So, even though they are Christian, because of some differences, like the names they use or the way they interpret a scripture, they will be attacked by some other fellow Christians and actually be denounced as non-Christians. The phrase "Hie to Kolob" just happens to tickle my funny bone, so for our purposes in this book, *Hie to Kolob* will be used as a term that is symbolic of the way two different people can interpret the same event or the way two minds can process the same thought stream differently.

Real estate agents, as in the previous example, may have similar passions for what they do but have different beliefs or realities as to which company structure and culture provides the best vehicle for service to their customers or clients and which will enable them to earn and keep the most money. Also entwined in the sales agent's belief system or reality is his or her position on what I will refer to as the "firm ←------→ sales agent continuum" of who is responsible for getting the listing or for making the sale. The firm ←------→ sales agent continuum is a measure of who is responsible for the business happening. Is it 80 percent the firm and 20 percent the sales agent? Is it 70 percent and 30 percent? Or 50 percent firm and 50 agent? Or 30 percent and 70 percent? 10 percent / 90 percent? 0 percent / 100 percent? Each sales agent will adopt a different reality on that continuum at different times in his or her career. I recently asked a small class of real estate agents and managers what their opinions were. The response was exactly what I expected. Those who were agents for 100 percent desk-fee offices each blurted out loudly and quickly "One hundred percent sales agent!" Those in traditional split offices responded more slowly with a variation from 20 percent firm and 80 percent sales agent all the way to 50 percent firm and 50 percent sales agent. Not one sales agent believed that the firm had more than 50 percent of the responsibility for the successes. The managers in attendance, however, varied from 70 percent firm and 30 percent sales agent to 50 percent each. It was also interesting for me to observe that the more time a manager had in that position, the more likely he or she was to claim more of the responsibility for the successes.

As the manager of the firm, you have certain systems of client services that are available for sales agents to plug themselves in to. Those systems that you, the manager, have in place will attract or repel sales agents, depending on the unique individual belief system that each sales agent has. The sales agent has three areas of concern when deciding on a new brokerage-firm affiliation or on a continued affiliation with your firm:

1) How much is the firm contributing to my success versus how much of my success is all me? (the firm ←------→ sales agent continuum)
2) What services will I be able to provide to my clients because of my affiliation with this firm and at what cost to me?
3) What services and conveniences are being provided to me by this firm, and at what cost to me?

The individual sales agent's answers to these questions will depend not just on his or her belief system but also on how the two belief systems (theirs and the firm's) fit or mesh together.

In other words, if the manager is trumpeting "Hie to Kolob," it will attract those with that belief system but repel all others. One particular sales agent I recently spoke with had a belief system based on her bachelor degree, ten years as an employee in an industry unrelated to real estate, eight months as a sales agent with a traditional commission split regional franchise, and four months with a 100 percent desk-fee brokerage firm. As she spoke, she spoke with unshakeable conviction. She *knew* the answers to the three questions and expressed them without any equivocation. "It is 100 percent all me! The brokerage or firm means nothing…does nothing for me, my clients, or my business."

Throughout my four weeks of conversation with her, she held firm to that belief system. Even when I introduced her to the possibility of other belief systems, she was unwilling to even consider that any other possibility could exist with any merit. Her facial expressions were ones of contempt as she spoke. She was clearly threatened by the mere mentioning of anything that didn't fall within the parameters of her own belief system. She is an intelligent person. She is a pleasant person. She is an energetic person. But as a manager of a brokerage or firm trying to recruit her to my systems of lead generation and company image, I would get nowhere with her. Arguably, I would assert here, that I could not ever convince her otherwise, no matter how logical and sensible it might seem to me, as a manager. I would have but two choices with her: provide a second business model that could operate simultaneously within my existing structure (which has inherent problems discussed in chapter 8) or not waste the energy but instead move on to find other sales agents who would embrace my business model and belief systems.

Let me illustrate this point from the other side. In the traditional commission split office I once owned and managed, I had a sales agent for ten years who rarely made under $100,000 in any given year. It seemed that her loyalty was so strong that I couldn't get her out of my company, no matter how hard I sometimes tried. She, admittedly, attributed 100 percent of her sales to the company name and to the company lead-generation programs. She would never have considered a 100 percent desk-fee type of firm where she would be responsible for generating her own leads. The manager of the 100 percent desk-fee office would be totally frustrated trying to convince her that "it is paradise and not Kolob." It just isn't within her belief system, and you're not going to change that, no matter how logical it may seem to you!

You see, there really isn't a right or a wrong business model. An owner or manager of a very large, independent, traditional commission split office once mused to me, "The desk-fee agents in this town like going around telling other agents and thinking in their own minds that they are 100 percent agents. By the time they pay all their own costs, including lead-generation, they are at best 60-40 commission split agents."

Within a week of hearing that, I listened to an owner of a 100 percent desk-fee office chortle, "How can agents at commission split offices be so stupid as to give all of those huge percentages of their commissions to their firm, when they could work here at my office and keep 100 percent of their sales commissions, with just a small monthly fee?"

See, it's just a matter of establishing a business model that fits your belief system, so that you have passion and conviction in what you do at the firm. The sales agents within your community who embrace your same, clearly defined belief system will be open to affiliation with your firm, answering the three questions previously posed.

One particular year, as a manager, my monthly budget for advertising in the local newspaper was $20,000. In an earlier special budget meeting, the seventy-five sales agents in the office had voted to assess themselves $65 each, per month, to expand that newspaper advertising budget even more, for an even greater impact in the community. As the manager, I had to have one of my subordinates take charge of the billing and collect from the sales agents. To say the least, it was a battle each month to collect that. That monthly total would have been $4,875, if it had ever been fully collected, which it never was. The company had to eat the shortage each month, have a salaried staff person do the collection, pay the company's normal $20,000, and run the mechanics of the program with the newspaper. Then, at the first of each new month, I had to run a check down to the newspaper for the previous month's bill. It was no easy task to pay that bill, and often we were short of funds, which made for a day of stressful scrambling to gather enough money so that we wouldn't be cut off by the newspaper running our advertisements. On one of those frantic days, a sales agent interrupted me to inform me of his displeasure with our newspaper presence! He said, "We [the agents] pay for it anyway, so why can't the office do more?" I was able to keep my cool and draw out on a piece of paper the company's monthly $20,000 versus the sales agents' $4,000 contribution versus his personal $65 contribution. He was shocked. His reality—his world—had never made that connection before. Hie to Kolob!

What specific trait or traits do you possess that are a handicap to your successful management? It is likely that those management handicaps are a result of the environment that you were born into. Likewise, your strengths are a result of the environment that you were born into. So, let's focus on "the handicap of your birth," as Anthony Robbins puts it. What was the emotional environment that you were born into? Which of the emotions was the most dominant in your surroundings? Fear? Jealousy? Hatred? Revenge? Greed? Anger? Explore, mentally, the intensity of the existence of each one of these emotions that prevailed in your birth environment, and then examine the effect that each of those has on you, right now, as a handicap to your successful leadership or management.

Popeye always says, "I yam what I yam!" Without outwardly professing it, the vast majority of people adhere to that philosophy. "I was born into this environment. This environment has made me this way." I yam what I yam. The thoughts and emotions that have handicapped you throughout your life are deeply embedded in your subconscious mind. It takes incredible effort to replace those negative thoughts and emotions that have formed your belief systems about your identity. There are voices, as Don Miguel Ruiz puts it in *The Voice of Knowledge* that speak to your mind, creating and confirming, over and over again, who you are…your identity. But they can be replaced. Who knows the exact odds of successfully doing that? It may be literally one in a million people who is able to shake the handicap of his or her birth and replace those emotions and thoughts (which form the belief system of your identity) with emotions and thoughts that will carry him or her to great heights of success. Show me the twenty most successful people in the world today, and I'll show you twenty people who each had to overcome the handicap of their birth with positive conscious thoughts and emotions that reconditioned their subconscious minds to allow their creative imaginations' thought streams to flow. Earlier in this book, I said that Stephen Covey's statement "Between stimulus and response there is choice" was only true at the conscious level of thinking. That is why we have to use our conscious mind to replace negative thoughts, emotions, and ultimately belief systems with positive ones.

As an example, I have always had a belief system that when people say to me, "Hello. How are you?" it is not a sincere, genuine question. They really, truly don't care how I am doing, so why ask? As a result of my pessimistic belief system, I always respond to "How are you?" with a straight facial expression and a curt, "Fine," or "Good." This is not something that a charismatic or personable person should be doing! I would like to be a more charismatic, personable individual, so I am now trying to consciously change my deeply entrenched, negative belief system of a lifetime by responding to that inquiry with "Terrific," "Fabulous," or "Fantastic." Over time, my hope is to replace the pessimistic feeling and subconscious thoughts of fear that no one really cares about me with a positive feeling and thoughts of acceptance, hope, and enthusiasm. In order for this transmutation to occur, I have to believe that it will happen and be consistent with my conscious efforts to smile and say, "Fabulous." If I can do that, that will be a huge stride in dealing with a personal handicap of my birth. It may take a long time, and I may need the help of family and friends to hold me accountable for these conscious actions, but by staying persistent with this discipline, I will change this old, damaging belief system!

What if your own damaging belief systems have already been cemented into your adaptive unconscious or subconscious mind as to what is fair, how hard you should work or not work, how much effort is reasonable, and so on. Your own belief systems are short-changing you! You are capable of doing so much more than you are now doing, but your own belief systems are creating a ceiling for you—not just a ceiling over what's fair for you to have to do (and no more) but a ceiling over your limitations. These voices, emotions, and belief systems of identity were created by a parent or parents who never reasoned with you but rather commanded, "Because I said so!" Parents so mired in their own dramas of work and life (that you were never engaged with them to learn basic survival and coping skills) have now left their imprint in your subconscious mind. Your limitations are inadvertently programmed into you and are now your belief systems. Those subconscious voices are telling you stories that your conscious mind isn't even aware of. "You can never leave the ghetto." "You can never make more than $75,000 a year." "You were meant to work for someone else." "You are not a leader; you are a follower." These voices from your deep subconscious mind repeat these (and worse) stories over and over, and it becomes the belief system that guides your every move! We severely underestimate the power of the subconscious mind. It carries out the program that the conscious mind has allowed to be created. It doesn't reason or judge; it just does!

In Napoleon Hill's classic book *Think and Grow Rich*, he explains how we all have both a synthetic imagination and a creative imagination, being separate faculties of the same mind. The faculty of the synthetic imagination creates nothing. "It merely works with the material of experience, education, and observation with which it is fed." Its limits are finite and therefore keep a sales agent working, thinking, and producing only what lies within the confines of that synthetic imagination. This is a belief system. It is not just a simple belief system but an incredibly powerful belief system. As I alluded to earlier, all extraordinary people have been able to break out of that faculty and have been able to use the creative imagination. "It is the faculty through which hunches and inspiration are received. It is by this faculty that basic or new ideas are developed." The creative imagination exists in all of us but lies dormant. It functions only when "the conscious mind is vibrating at an exceedingly rapid rate, as for example when the conscious mind is stimulated through the emotion of strong desire." It is like the muscles in your body that grow and become stronger with use but become dormant when not used. The creative imagination needs to be exercised, stimulated, and activated. It is the great manager's task to play upon those forces within each sales agent's mind that will activate both the synthetic and the creative imaginations. The sales agent's intangible desire to generate income can be given concrete form through the creative imagination. The creative imagination is a major component of the adaptive unconscious or subconscious mind. Whatever we call it, it is real! It will generate more income for the sales agent than will any commission split or office perk. Consider these words from Napoleon Hill:

> The earth, every one of the individual cells of your body and every atom of matter began as an intangible form of energy. Desire is a thought impulse! Thought impulses are forms of energy. When you begin with the thought impulse desire to accumulate money, you are drafting into your service the same "stuff" that nature used in creating this earth and every material form in the universe, including the body and brain in which the thought impulses function. As far as science has been able to determine, the entire universe consists of but two elements—matter and energy. Through the combination of energy and matter has been created everything perceptible…

Those intangible thoughts and desires for success can become reality when the right energy is applied, in the right way. The great manager of an office or company knows how to apply pressures through internal office systems that will bring out the true potential of the sales agent, with the main stimulant for the creative imagination (subconscious mind) being accountability. In chapter 4, "Accountability," we will explore some specific systems for an office environment and culture that will act as stimulants for the creative imaginations of sales agents.

As the manager, you are the heart of the company. You can employ certain systems, creating a culture in your office that is conducive to bringing out the maximum potential of each sales agent who is willing to submit to your systems, but you cannot change the behaviors of those who will not submit to the stimulants (office systems) that bring out their best. So changing a sales agent's behavior is no guarantee, but the one (and most important) person whose behavior you can change is your own! As the heart of the company, those changes that you make on a constant basis begin to flow through your organization like blood flowing through healthy veins. You are the heart pumping that blood. As we explore each of these vital six belief systems, look first at the relevance to you personally and then to those you employ. Don't get caught up in the distractions of the name *heaven* versus the name *Kolob*. Make yourself healthy with healthy belief systems, and there will be a natural following of sales agents and staff that will mesh with your belief systems and ultimately create the culture that you desire within your company.

In 1980 a movie called *The Elephant Man* was released, and I remember excitedly rushing out to watch it at the theater. It was based on the true story of Joseph Merrick (called John Merrick in the movie), who was born with a disease that left him hideously deformed by the age of three or four. In the movie, he was sold to a circus owner, called Bytes, who used him as a sideshow. People would pay to look at him in his cage. Children and adults alike would point and laugh at him with derision, talking openly about his freakish appearance. The circus owner treated him like an animal. The difficulty that he had in moving around, because of his huge head and other deformities, left him feeling like he really was an animal. His identity was that he was a freak—an animal. That identity was pounded into him every moment of every day. He had no one and nothing to tell him otherwise. He was the elephant man—a freak show.

A doctor named Frederick Treves went to the circus and saw the elephant man sideshow. He could see how sick Joseph (John) Merrick was and could sense the human element within that creature known as the elephant man. Doctor Treves tried to give help but was briskly dismissed by the circus owner. He was finally purchased by the good doctor. Merrick was given comfort and medical care. Doctor Treves soon discovered that Merrick wasn't mute at all and that he could read and write and was spiritual and intelligent. Treves's heart broke as he realized that Merrick had endured all those years suffering indignity and stripped of his identity as a man, having instead to have an identity as a freakish animal forced upon him. The circus owner, Bytes, tried to take his star sideshow back, resulting in a scene with Merrick running through the street being chased by a gang of young men. They cornered him and ripped off his facial mask that he wore in public. That was when Merrick so emotionally cried out, "I am not an animal! I am a human being! I…am…a *man*! It is gripping to see him fight to claim his true identity against all odds. The movie was nominated for eight Academy Awards.

As individuals, when we try to form our own realities, to live our own dream, outside of the dream that others have imposed upon us, other people can feel so offended and assaulted by our deviation from their agenda that they will sometimes become quiet character assassins. The very people who claim to love us can react to our life's choices with viciousness reminiscent of Bytes, the circus owner in *The Elephant Man*. Anyone who has ever had to deal with character attacks (where others try to rewrite your identity through gossip) know the feeling of wanting to cry out, "I am not an animal! I am a human being! I…am…a man!" The reason that I bring up the individual aspect of identity is that unless you understand this concept on a personal level, you cannot understand the importance of your company identity.

In the fall of 2011, I was hired to be the compliance and coaching arm of a company that I watched grow from about 80 sales associates to more than 270 in a four-year span. As I watched the growth, I also watched fallout of agents leaving the company and have concluded that the fallout was as necessary as the hires. The owners had conclusively decided what the culture of their company was going to be, and when sales agents joined but clashed with the culture (like oil and water), it led those agents to leave and simultaneously strengthened the belief systems of the owners and of the sales agents who were culturally in step. It was a cleansing of sorts. I watched sales agents enter and try to manipulate and force the company to conform to their realities, which clashed with the company culture, and it only led to the sales agents' frustration and eventual departure. Every departure was treated respectfully with well wishes for that agent's success elsewhere, which, ironically, was part of the culture.

Each individual is unique. Each individual has genetic differences and has a different environment where he or she is raised and taught. Each individual has different experiences and interprets events in life differently. I can guarantee you that you don't know what it's like to be me. Yet, as we talk to each other, you can start to get a feel as to whether or not you and I could work well together. If not, it doesn't make either of us bad or good… just different.

If your business model differs from the norm in your market, you will be subject to others trying to rewrite your company identity, engaging in character assassination (Hie to Kolob!). As the manager, you must be resolute in knowing who you are as a company. Whether it's a franchise banner you're waving or a small, independent banner, a 100 percent desk-fee banner or a traditional split office banner, you have to wave that banner high in the air, with pride, in spite of how it may rock the realities of other people's worlds. The company culture, though formed by the discussed belief systems, begins and ends with the manager's adherence to the company's true identity. With that said, now let's take a look at the six belief systems that will be your company culture.

4

Say What You'll Do; Do What You Say; Prove It
(Accountability)

E xamine yourself for a moment. If I ask you to describe a great leader to me, what do you say? Go ahead and say it out loud, right now, as an exercise. So that you can't equivocate from your initial response, say it out loud, right now. What specific individuals' faces or images sprang into your mind? Your initial reaction to my question is likely your current belief system of a great leader. It is based on the stimuli that have surrounded you in your lifetime. Those descriptions and mental images of great leaders that you have in your mind are probably outwardly observable qualities, such as a strong voice, a loud voice, steely eyes, energetic facial expressions, and so on.

Within most people's reality or belief system is an image of a successful leader that is loud, commanding, rigid, humorless, brazen, proud, and self-assured. When you think of US presidents, most of them would fit into that mold. Abraham Lincoln probably stands alone as a very humble, soft-spoken president. What many don't realize, though, is that inside him was burning an incredible resolve to lay the foundation for an enduring great nation, even though he was faced with a constitutional crisis and threat of a split union. His outwardly calm and humble persona masked an inwardly intense and energetic individual. In Jim Collins' book *Good to Great*, he isolates eleven companies (out of over 1,400 good companies) as great. The leader, CEO, of each had that combination of humility and intense resolve that President Lincoln also possessed. This thought intrigued me, perhaps because I am a soft-spoken and humble individual (and proud of it!). But as I have spent much time pondering this concept, I realize that I clearly lack the inner resolve and the true humility that the great leaders possess. I also realize that my own belief systems held the image of a great leader being somewhat like Foghorn Leghorn of cartoon fame.

In Captain Michael Abrashoff's book *It's Your Ship*, he delves into the age-old belief system of a great leader and then artfully dispels those myths, making the Foghorn Leghorn irrelevant as a leader. Abrashoff learned, among many other things, to ask himself three questions before confronting a problem. He would swallow his temper, turn inward for the solution (as opposed to blaming someone else), and ask the following:

1) Did I clearly articulate the goals?
2) Did I give people enough time and resources to accomplish the task?
3) Did I give them enough training?

That's a far cry from what most of us would instinctively do when we are feeling criticized. We try to deflect blame onto another with a humiliation of him or her or a blame tantrum. Most Foghorn Leghorns would quickly put a subordinate in his or her place, deflect all personal responsibility for the problem, and do it all very loudly and forcefully to make people think, "He must be right. After all, he is very loud and authoritarian." People's senses of fairness and justice become piqued by this type of leadership, and mutiny is sure to follow. They will eventually see through the facade of loudness and seek resolve. Captain Abrashoff's three self-addressed questions give rise to a true understanding and a truer conviction of the answer.

This doesn't mean, of course, that you as the manager take all the blame, but it does require that you allow yourself to be held accountable and to have your own job performance evaluated. It also requires that the manager holds each employee and salesperson accountable. Captain Abrashoff also says,

I gave consistent feedback at regular intervals throughout the year, formally on a quarterly basis, but also as part of the daily routine. Whenever people did something great, I let them know. Whenever they came up short, I did not let it fester until the end of the evaluation period; I got it out in the open right away."

No one likes being involved in an adversarial or confrontational situation, but from time to time it's inevitable. That's why we get paid the big bucks. Don't try to hide behind anyone else. Stand up to the plate.

When it is time to inform the bottom performers that, in fact, that's what they are, I have found that asking them how they would rate their own performances is effective. Most recognize that in relation to their peers, they are at the bottom of the curve.

Whenever I had deficient performers, I always laid out a game plan for them to improve. I'd bring them in, tell them what their problems were, what they needed to do to correct them, and provide training if they needed it. I would give them a deadline by which I expected them to have their deficiencies corrected. If necessary, I would clearly lay out in advance what would happen if they didn't.

I'm proud that I didn't have to fire or reassign anyone, but I was prepared to do so if I had to. All managers must be ready to shed poor performers, but only after you have given them every chance; you must be open and honest with them, clarify their deficiencies and how they can overcome them. And finally, you must spell out the stick: what will happen if they don't address those problems in a timely manner.

Not every manager has the ability to follow through and apply the consequences to the poor action or inaction. But it must be done by someone. The message is sent out to the masses of what you will or will not tolerate. A great manager must have an emotional skin that is thick enough to hold people accountable.

So, maybe the first step to take toward being a better manager, through understanding belief systems, is to change some of your own long-held beliefs. You have to make definite, stubborn, conscious efforts to replace long-established subconscious beliefs. The chances are pretty good that you know yourself—your strengths and your weaknesses. Based on your belief systems, some of the traits that you put into the strength category might be placed in the weakness category from other people's perspective by their observations of you. And the reverse of that is also true. In actuality, for every weakness that an individual or company possesses, there are strengths that stem from it. And for every strength that an individual or company possesses, there are weaknesses that stem from it.

For example, I asked a retail manager to name her greatest strength. She said that she got along like a best friend with every employee. Then before I could ask her what weaknesses stemmed from that strength, she blurted out that employees all took advantage of her friendship and used her to get what they wanted and to "get away with stuff." She then said, "It would be better for a manager to be a cold bitch." Her own perception of what constitutes a good manager's quality changed in the course of seconds. Now, it was irrelevant to her that the "cold bitch's" weakness would be that no one in the company would feel important or at home within the company. Take a good, hard look at your well-thought-out list of your personal strengths and your list of your weaknesses. Think of the opposite by-product of each itemized strength and weakness. Do the same exercise with your company that you manage.

Holding your employees and sales agents accountable and allowing your staff to hold you accountable create a culture of discipline. The way that you, the employer, should hold your staff (both employees and sales agents) accountable is as follows. *First*, have a minimum standard for production or performance. Anything less than that standard will not be tolerated. Performing below your company's minimum standard must result in termination from the company or, in the alternative, placement into a time-sensitive probation program that is micromanaged. The concept is, of course, nothing new. But the dogged follow-through on accountability is. We will see shortly how this often-ignored holding their feet to the fire forms the psychological foundation for the culture of the company. *Second*, each individual in your employ must have an initial business planning meeting where personal goals must be set. The goals need to stretch them out of the limits and confines of their current belief system. In other words, they set *big, hairy, audacious goals* (BHAGs) with your counsel, so that their subconscious mind or creative imagination can begin to create their new reality, using matter and energy. The tighter (more frequent) your follow-up is, the more effective it will be. As this new reality of theirs is visited by their conscious mind on a daily basis (or in some cases, multiple times each day), it begins to drip into the subconscious mind, causing massive behavioral changes—belief system changes that result in action.

As a fairly new managing broker and owner of a (forty salespeople at that time) real estate brokerage, I had been trying to break the one-million-dollar mark for annual gross commissions earned by the office. My quest began in 1987 in a county with only three or four out of about sixty real estate brokerages making that much. For me, it was a lofty goal, which I spent the next decade building up, and the whole time frustratingly bumping my head up against this glass ceiling I had set (and set up as a limitation, without knowing it). My finite mind couldn't conceive of more. In 1998, I had a great master of human thinking named Lou Tice tell me about my finite limitations I had been creating for myself with this *easy* goal. Then, at a convention that year, I heard both Arnold Schwarzenegger and Anthony Robbins speak, and in their own ways, they addressed this same issue. I accepted the challenge that they had each made to at least double my previous year's goal for the coming year. The challenge included a focus on psychological acceptance of the goal without any initial specific plan and letting the subconscious mind (driven by the goal) create the plan of action. On a logical level, it did not make sense to me, but I committed to exercise faith in the concept and trust that my subconscious mind would create.

About two-thirds of the way through the year, with only a slight glimmer of hope that my office would even make the one-million-dollar let alone the two-million-dollar mark, a knock came on the door of my personal residence late one night. It was a discouraged competitor who had been performing about 50 percent more gross sales with his company than I was with mine. His negative cash flow had beaten down his will to the point that he was now ready to just walk away from his company and let me see if I could manage the cash flow that had been an insurmountable obstacle for him for too many years. On the outside, no one would have known that his forty-plus agent office with wonderful gross sales volume had been spending more than it brought in. It was a tailor-made acquisition. That year, my company, with its new acquisition, made 1.8 million dollars in gross commissions but, even more important, shattered the glass ceiling that I had psychologically set up for myself as my company did 3.3 million dollars in gross commission income two years later and 5 million just two years after that.

Looking back on the acquisition year, I can now understand why it was important for me to seek out and build good relationships with my fellow managing brokers in my town even though, at that time, I couldn't consciously understand my own behavior. My competing fellow managers must have really thought I was nuts! It was only crazy behavior to the logical finite mind that had not yet been given the mandate to create by the powerful subconscious. Look at the historic milestone of Roger Bannister breaking the four-minute-mile in 1954. Previous to his achievement, no one in history had run a mile in under four minutes. In history! I'm sure that there were many athletes throughout time who were more committed, in better shape, or more gifted as runners. But Bannister was able to shatter a psychological ceiling. Over the next year, after he broke that psychological ceiling, thirty-seven more people broke the four-minute barrier. The next year after that, three hundred people broke it. There was not a sudden physical breakthrough or a new strain of superhumans born in the 1930s. It was a mental glass ceiling over the world, established by humans' finite thinking. Roger Bannister's greatness was his ability to conquer the limitations of his own mind, which had been set by society.

Yes, the natural defense mechanisms of the sales agent's mind will resist and fight against this as an illegitimate notion of hype and mumbo jumbo. To the successful businessperson, it is as logical as any other system or routine within his or her business model. Getting the sales agents to accept this concept is essential in getting them to accept accountability. When they understand the logic (and consciously accept that accountability is as important as any of their sales tools and dialogues), you will maximize their sales potential. Help them to understand with examples that they can relate to, such as the following: You are driving along in your car, and you are so caught up in a conscious preoccupation, worry, or problem that you zone out. Before long, you snap out of it, realizing that you have been driving several miles without even being consciously aware! Your subconscious mind was driving the car while your conscious mind was deep in thought! Or the basketball player who gets in a zone, shooting the ball—he or she just knows that the ball will go in when it is shot. The subconscious mind has taken over! Think of the golfer whose negative self-talk has been so strong for so long that as he or she brings the golf club back to hit the ball off the tee, the subconscious mind changes the grip or drops the elbow or whatever it needs to do to mess up the stroke, fulfilling the mandate he or she has been feeding to that obedient subconscious mind! Remember, the subconscious mind doesn't discern between good and bad or right and wrong. It just carries out the messages that the conscious mind has given to it.

In Anthony Robbins's book *Awaken the Giant Within*, he explains the logic behind this principle as follows:

What is this seemingly extrasensory perception they have to notice anything and everything that relates to their goal or can be used to achieve their heart's desire? I believe that in each case, these individuals have learned to use a mechanism in their brains known as the Reticular Activating System.

It sounds complex, and undoubtedly the actual process is, but the function of your RAS is simple and profound; it determines what you will notice and what you will pay attention to. It is the screening device of your mind. Remember that your conscious mind can focus only on a limited number of elements at any one time, so your brain expends a lot of effort deciding what not to pay attention to. There are countless stimuli bombarding you right now, but your brain deletes most of it and focuses on what you believe is important. Its mechanism for achieving this is the RAS. Thus your RAS is directly responsible for how much of reality you consciously experience.

Let me offer you an example. Have you ever bought a new outfit or car, and then suddenly notice it everywhere you looked? Why was that? Didn't they exist before? Yes, of course they did, but you're noticing them now because your purchase of this item was a clear demonstration to your RAS that anything related to this object is now significant and needs to be noticed. You have an immediate and heightened awareness of something that actually has always been around you.

This shift in mental posture aligns you more precisely with your goals. Once you decide that something is a priority, you give it tremendous emotional intensity, and by continually focusing on it, any resource that supports its attainment will eventually become clear. Therefore, it's not crucial to understand exactly how you'll achieve your goals when you first set them. Trust that your RAS will point out what you need to know along the way.

When the conscious human mind is faced with a task that is finite and limited realms cannot come to resolution with (whether out of fear, a feeling of inadequacy, or simply not understanding the how), it wanders down sometimes strange paths to bring conclusion and resolution. Young adults, for example, faced with the daunting task of providing for their own lifestyles (which they've become accustomed to in their parents' home), which were always provided for them (up to that point), are forced to leave a carefree "que sera sera" way of thinking and seriously focus on college, career paths, debt, and other responsibilities for the first time. Perhaps they'll feel no fear, at first, because their belief system of entitlement or their warped sense of fairness has them assuming that their parents or society's taxes will pay for everything and they need not make adjustments in lifestyle. The sad reality will set in later. Or perhaps they will face these realities with confidence and excitement, taking on those challenges of paying for education and other living expenses, studying, following a career path, and making lifestyle choices to live within a budget. (All parents hope for that one.) The third alternative for the young adult is that the stress of the young mind (controlled by fear, feelings of inadequacy, or not understanding the how) will cause it to break from reality and slip into mental states, ranging from depression to schizophrenia, depending on the makeup of that individual brain and the preparedness of the young mind for those challenges. But when there is no way of going back to childhood, one of those three alternatives occurs (the first being a simple delay of the decision). Individual accountability forces the individual to move forward, and the strong survive. American society has some safety nets for those who don't.

But in managing your business, you cannot take on the role of social engineer. You must apply this harsh accountability tool of nature to your business—survive or perish! "Burn the boats!" The ancient Greeks were known for doing this in war. As they would land their boats onto the enemy's beaches, the commander would burn the boats so that the soldiers were given no possibility of retreat—conquer or perish! Hernan Cortez did the same thing when he left the island of Cuba to go to mainland Mexico for the purpose of conquering the Aztecs and obtaining their gold. Upon landing, he had the boats burned in front of his soldiers so that they all understood that there was no going back, no retreating on anyone's part—conquer or perish! This is the most powerful accountability tool for the management of your business—perform or get out! Your salespeople's minds will try desperately to find escapes from the harsh accountability, but you can't allow an out. You must terminate them from your employ, without excuse, if they do not perform to clearly defined expectations.

This concept also brings to mind the incredibly brave and honorable fifty-six men who signed the Declaration of Independence. Yes, prior to July 4, 1776, there had been some heroic acts by Thomas Jefferson, Patrick Henry, Richard Henry Lee, John Hancock, and others, but to me, these rumblings of heroism were just a prelude to the ultimate accountability of signing their own death warrant, for them and for their families, when they signed the Declaration of Independence. By publicly attaching their names to this treasonous act, they ensured that the British would hang them, and they knew it! There was no retreating at that point, no going back. It was the ultimate accountability—victory or death!

When I first started in real estate sales, I was financially supporting a wife and two baby boys. I had put my application in at the co-op that did the hiring for public schoolteachers in secondary education. It was my fallback in case real estate sales didn't work out. I got by (barely) for nearly three years but then had a series of transactions fall through under bizarre circumstances. As if fate were calling, I received a phone call from the hiring co-op, rushed out to an interview, and was immediately hired for a full-time teaching job at a nearby high school. It felt perfect, and I felt so relieved. But that night, I struggled with the thought of a life in the public school system and throwing away the foundation I had just laid for a real estate career. After long, anguishing deliberation, I called the co-op the next day and withdrew my job acceptance. I was told by the co-op that I was burning my bridges and could never return to the public school system there. I told them that I understood. There was now no retreat for me where there had previously been that fallback. The next three months were incredible! I closed as much in sales in those three months as I had in the previous three years combined! Succeed or perish creates a strong accountability when there are no fallbacks and the manager allows that natural accountability to take place.

In Malcolm Gladwell's book *Outliers*, he chronicles the success of a junior high school in the Bronx that brought out the best in students through accountability. As I recount his story, look at the many parallels between what KIPP has done and what should be done in a business to bring the same result.

In the mid-1990s, an experimental public school called the KIPP Academy opened on the fourth floor of Lou Gehrig junior high school in New York City. Lou Gehrig is in the seventh school district, otherwise known as the South Bronx, one of the poorest neighborhoods in New York City. It is a squat, gray 1960s-era building across the street from a bleak-looking group of high-rises. A few blocks over is Grand Concourse, the borough's main thoroughfare. These are not streets that you'd happily walk down, alone, after dark.

KIPP is a middle school. Classes are large: the fifth grade has two sections of thirty-five students each. There are no entrance exams or admissions requirements. Students are chosen by lottery, with any fourth grader living in the Bronx eligible to apply. Roughly half of the students are African American; the rest are Hispanic. Three-quarters of the children come from single-parent homes. Ninety percent qualify for "free or reduced lunch," which is to say that their families earn so little that the federal government chips in so the children can eat properly at lunchtime.

KIPP Academy seems like the kind of school in the kind of neighborhood with the kind of student that would make educators despair—except that the minute you enter the building, it's clear that something is different. The students walk quietly down the hallways in single file. In the classroom, they are taught to turn and address anyone talking to them in a protocol known as "SSLANT": smile, sit up, listen, ask questions, nod when being spoken to, and track with your eyes. On the walls of the school's corridors are hundreds of pennants from the colleges that KIPP graduates have gone on to attend. Last year, hundreds of families from across the Bronx entered the lottery for KIPP's two fifth-grade classes. It is no exaggeration to say that just over ten years into its existence, KIPP has become one of the most desirable public schools in New York City.

What KIPP is most famous for is mathematics. In the South Bronx, only about 16 percent of all middle school students are performing at or above their grade level in math. But at KIPP, by the end of the fifth grade, many of the students call math their favorite subject. In the seventh grade, KIPP students start high school algebra. By the end of eighth grade, 84 percent of the students are performing at or above their grade level, which is to say that this motley group of randomly chosen lower-income kids from dingy apartments in one of the country's worst neighborhoods—whose parents, in an overwhelming number of cases, never set foot in a college—do as well in mathematics as the privileged eighth graders of America's wealthy suburbs. "Our kid's reading is on point," said David Levin, who founded KIPP with a fellow teacher, Michael Feinberg, in 1994. "They struggle a little bit with writing skills. But when they leave here, they rock in math."

"They start school at seven twenty-five," says David Levin of the students at the Bronx KIPP Academy. "They all do a course called thinking skills until seven thirty-five. They do ninety minutes of English, ninety minutes of math every day, except in fifth grade, where they do two hours of math every day. An hour of science, an hour of social science, an hour of music at least twice a week, and then you have an hour and fifteen minutes of orchestra on top of that. Everyone does orchestra. The day goes from 7:25 until 5:00 p.m. After five, there are homework clubs, detention, sports teams. There are kids here from 7:25 until 7:00 p.m. If you take an average day, and you take out lunch and recess, our kids are spending 50 to 60 percent more time learning than the traditional public school student."

Levin was standing in the school's main hallway. It was lunchtime and the students were trooping by quietly in orderly lines, all of them in their KIPP Academy shirts. Levin stopped a girl whose shirttail was out. "Do me a favor, when you get a chance," he called out, miming a tuck-in movement. He continued, "Saturdays they come in nine to one. In the summer, it's eight to two." By summer, Levin was referring to the fact that KIPP students do three extra weeks of school, in July…

"The beginning is hard," he went on. "By the end of the day they're restless. Part of it is endurance, part of it is motivation. Part of it is incentives and rewards and fun stuff. Part of it is good old fashioned discipline. You throw all of that into the stew. We talk a lot here about grit and self-control. The kids know what those words mean."

You get the picture. This enormous success story has happened because the students "see the clear relationship between effort and reward." KIPP promises that it will take kids who are stuck in poverty and give them a chance to get out. It will get 84 percent of them up or above their grade level in mathematics. Ninety percent of KIPP students get scholarships to private or parochial high schools. More than 80 percent of KIPP graduates will go on to college. They see the vision of who they can be and that it is possible, and they are willing to pay the price to get it. Waking up at 5:30 to 6:00 to start a disciplined day that won't end until late that evening, that's the price. Now, let's translate all of that to management of people in business.

Why shouldn't your company run like the KIPP Academy? Those kids don't have to put up with a rigorous schedule. But if they don't, they are terminated from the program. If they are terminated from the program, they will be consigned to a life that will go nowhere. It's a reality that causes those kids great pain, intellectually and emotionally. They are held accountable to perform their tasks, and they anticipate the rewards of their perseverance. The anticipated results of their perseverance are both physical and internal (intellectual and emotional). MRI tests have shown that the pleasure center of the brain lights up with activity through the anticipation of meaningful rewards. What is meaningful is different for everybody, so as the manager, it is important to have systems of anticipated pain and systems of anticipated pleasure in your office environment that will reach across the spectrum of variation in your salespeople. Doctor Dick McKenna, a management trainer for Century 21 for many years, referred to these as "push and pull pressures." Push pressures will create the dread anticipation of pain, and pull pressures will create the ecstatic anticipation of pleasure. You set up the systems, and you must hold each person accountable. Here are some systems that I found to work well:

Push Pressures (Pain)

1.) Company minimum production standard—An example might be that each sales agent must obtain a minimum of one sale written or one new listed property each month. Or each agent must close a minimum of $45,000 in gross closed commissions each year. The consequence is termination or possibly being put on a probationary status while being subjected to a back-to-basics program. Ouch!

2.) A real estate brokerage manager must have a visible, effective system for recruiting sales agents to the office, either newly licensed, experienced, or both. Once, in a crowded 3,800-square-foot office with thirty-five desks, I had seventy sales agents. At a sales meeting, I announced that I anticipated another six to ten sales agents joining our team over the next week or two. As I spoke, I watched the faces and expressions of the sales agents. The productive agents looked pleased…unfazed. The unproductive agents looked bewildered. I could read their lips, "Where will he put them?" It didn't take long before they realized what it meant for them: produce or get out! It is an incredibly powerful psychological tool for pushing the low producers along. Yes, it hurts, and the anticipation of that pain is agonizing!

3.) Hold quarterly accountability sessions with each agent. For the high producer, it is short and sweet. For the low producer, it is pain—to have to have their low numbers looking them right in the eyes. (You might call it a "business planning session").

4.) In your "wants and needs" sharing sessions of sales meetings, make each person talk, in turn, by either saying "pass" or telling of their new listing, new sale, price reduction, or other significant activity. Making people say "pass" is painful for them. It means they've got nothing going on! They will start looking for excuses for not attending. You must hold them accountable and not let them escape their obligation to attend. It will force their creative imagination of their subconscious mind to create business or in the alternative to leave your employ. Either way, it's the best thing for them…and your company!

5.) Print out a monthly report showing the sequential gross closed commissions, year to date. Don't show names next to the amounts. Just number them by rankings in the office, and at the bottom of the page, say, "You are number thirty-five on the list." It looks them right in the eyes and sets the subconscious mind to work.

These "push pressures" each have powerful psychological undercurrents that will cause the sales agent to frantically seek escape. They'll try to hide, hoping you won't notice or that you won't have the courage to terminate them from your employ. You must be relentless in holding them accountable. The pain will cause them to either leave your company or, if they are courageous, to submit to the pressure, which will cause their mind to begin creating a new way of being.

Pull Pressures (Rewards)

1.) Awards and recognition—For many people, this is a bigger motivator than money. To be presented a trophy or plaque in front of one's peers can serve as a great reward for many. The awards can be either for production or for customer service or both.

2.) The monthly production report referred to in item number 5 above is also a great motivator for many. The thrill of competition drives many of us to greater heights, as we try month after month to improve our office standing.

3.) Parties and social events, given as rewards for achievement of team goals can motivate many.

4.) Special privileges or gifts for short-term accomplishments, meted consistently, can add to the atmosphere of motivation.

5.) Using positions and titles and physical desk and work station placements, based on production, also contributes greatly to serving as a reward system.

It is not any one item that will serve as the pleasure or reward, but rather it is a combination of these things that creates a culture within your office. With push and pull pressures (pain and reward) being applied consistently, the accountability is an automaton. It drives the behaviors, and the manager just has to make sure that each system is being followed through with.

Glaringly absent from the reward list is bonuses and higher commission splits. *These are not motivators!* The sales agent's conscious mind will try to make a case for them, and you may unwittingly buy in to this idea, but it isn't true. Consider Ori and Rom Brafman's account of the Swiss government's disposal of nuclear waste from their book *Sway*:

In the 1940s, alarmed by the atrocities of World War II, Switzerland's political leaders began developing a nuclear program. In typical Swiss fashion, the program priorities soon shifted to the more peaceful goal of creating nuclear power: five plants now provide about 40 percent of Switzerland's electricity. The country has a relatively clean energy program, but with any nuclear power comes nuclear waste—waste that has to go somewhere.

In 1993, the Swiss government identified two small towns as potential nuclear waste depositories, but they didn't know how the townspeople would react. Would they be outraged? Or, by understanding the importance of the nation's nuclear energy program, would they take one for the team?

Two University of Zurich researchers were equally curious and decided to try to get some answers to this question. They asked the residents of the towns: "Suppose that the National Cooperative for the Storage of Radioactive waste (NAGRA), after completing exploratory drilling, proposed to build the repository for low and midlevel radioactive waste in your hometown. Federal experts examined this proposition, and the federal parliament decides to build the repository in your community." In a town hall meeting, the townspeople were asked whether they would accept this proposition or reject it.

Naturally, many people were frightened by the prospect of having the waste facility so close to their homes. But at the same time, whether out of social obligation, or a feeling of national pride, or just a sense that it was the fair thing to do, 50.8 percent of respondents agreed to put themselves at risk for the common good. The other half of the respondents, however—those who said they would oppose the facility—still represented a significant obstacle for the government.

To see if this problem could be resolved, the researchers tested out a seemingly rational solution to bring the nuclear waste dump opponents on board. They talked to a new group of individuals from the same community and presented them with the same scenario, but added, "Moreover, the parliament decides to compensate all residents of the host community with 5,000 francs (about $2,175) per year and per person…financed by all taxpayers in Switzerland." Once again they were asked, in a town hall meeting, would they accept this proposition or reject it?

Now, from an economic perspective, a monetary incentive should make the proposition of living close to a nuclear waste storage facility easier to swallow. Indeed, we naturally assume that the best way to get someone to do something unpleasant or difficult is to offer some kind of financial incentive. It's why employers give bonuses when their employees take on more challenging or time-consuming work and why parents tie their children's allowances to performance of specific chores. Along this line of reasoning, the higher the compensation, the more likely it should be that people would do what you were paying them for.

Regardless of how much money is actually offered, though, rationally speaking, any amount of money should be better than nothing at all. That is, the $2,175 the Swiss researchers proposed might not be enough to convince all residents, but it could win over at least some of those who were opposed.

But that's not what happened.

For some reason, when the researchers introduced financial compensation into the equation, the percentage of people who said they would accept the proposition not only didn't increase—it fell by half. Instead of being motivated by the financial incentive, the townspeople were swayed to reject the nuclear dump en masse: only 24.6 percent of the people who were presented with the monetary offer agreed to have the nuclear dump close to their town (compared with the 50.8 percent who agreed when no money was offered). In addition to contradicting the laws of economic theory, this response just doesn't make sense.

Even when the researchers sweetened the deal to $4,350—and then again to $6,525—the locals remained firm in their opposition. Only a single respondent, in fact, changed his mind and accepted the offer when more money was put on the table.

Managers, parents, and, of course, economists have long operated under the assumption that monetary incentives increase motivation. But psychologists are beginning to discover that the connection between the two is trickier than it first appears.

And I used to wonder why it was that whenever I did a sales contest or offered commission or bonus incentives, it never worked! It's not a huge motivator! I have personally been motivated, many times, after hearing an inspirational speaker or reading an inspirational thought. It would only move me so far and for so long though. Then, with the seemingly overwhelming circumstances of life, I would lose those once-fresh motivations. I do not believe that I am unique in this dilemma. Almost all human beings, while once fired up to do, accomplish, or be something, will have that conscious focus interrupted. They will go off their diet, start smoking again, or stop prospecting sales calls. Whatever the original, well-intentioned goal was, it will eventually be derailed. Thus a manager's challenge is to motivate salespeople and keep them motivated long term.

The nucleus accumbens is commonly called the pleasure center of the brain. In *Sway*, the Brafmans write, "At its most extreme, the pleasure center drives addiction. A drug like Cocaine, for example, triggers the nucleus accumbens to release dopamine, which creates a feeling of contentment and ecstasy. The reason cocaine is so addictive is that the pleasure center goes into overdrive and the threshold for excitement climbs higher and higher. The MRI study surprised the researchers because it revealed that the pleasure center is also where we react to financial compensation. And the more money there is on the line, the more the pleasure center lights up. A monetary reward is—biologically speaking—like a tiny line of cocaine."

Another totally separate part of the brain from the nucleus accumbens, or pleasure center, is the posterior superior temporal sulcus, commonly called the altruism center. It lights up on the MRI when there is a feeling of doing a common good. The Brafman book continues, "It's as if we have two 'engines' running in our brains that can't operate simultaneously. We can approach a task either altruistically or from a self-interest perspective. The two different engines run on different fuels and also need different amounts of those fuels to fire up. It doesn't take much to fuel the altruism center; all you need is the sense that you're helping someone or making a positive impact."

The pleasure center needs a certain amount; it needs the anticipation of a certain amount, which varies from person to person, and it may undermine the altruism center altogether. "Neuropsychologists have shown that activities associated with addictive substances and those associated with monetary reward are both processed by the pleasure center. Because monetary pleasures present such a strong allure to us, they distort our thinking." Working in real estate sales, for example, this concept doesn't mean that the anticipation of earning commissions doesn't work to drive behavior. It just isn't all that relevant what the commission split is or how much the bonus is. That subject is reserved for the belief system of fairness and justice (which we will discuss in chapter 6) and seems to be driven by the altruism center of the brain.

Continuing with the Brafmans, "Now the problem isn't with rewards per se. It's only when you dangle the possibility of reward ahead of time— creating a quid pro quo situation—that these destructive effects arise. An external review and analysis of motivation studies found that the prospect of a reward excites the pleasure center even more than the attainment itself. Taking a kid to Disneyland because she won the science fair is one thing, but telling her ahead of time, 'If you enter the fair and win it, I'll take you to Disneyland,' is another. It's that anticipation factor that drives the addictive behavior and suppresses the altruism center."

So, the anticipation of receiving commissions for closing sales is a definite driving force, affecting the pleasure center of the brain. But it is in the anticipation of the commission. Once it is received, it seems that the sales agent loses the high and begins to weigh out the fairness and justice of the whole thing.

For many years, it has been widely accepted that Abraham Maslow's hierarchy of needs was the key. At the low end of those needs are the biological and physiological needs, such as air, food, water, shelter, sleep, and so on. Until those needs are met, people feel no motivation to do anything else. But once met, they can move up to safety and security needs, like protection, law, order, stability, limits, and so on. Only then can they graduate to social needs, like family, affection, relationships, and so on. From there, they move up to ego or esteem needs, such as achievements, status, responsibility, and reputation. The highest of all of Maslow's hierarchy of needs is self-actualization. This last step is general growth and fulfillment. Conventional wisdom told a manager that unless those first two levels of Maslow's hierarchy were fulfilled, people could not move on to successful sales careers, and "draws on commissions" type programs were toyed with to fill that void. Often, they asked initial interview questions like, "Do you have enough money to sustain you for at least six months without any income?"

Emphasis has also been placed on a solid foundation of policies and rules (structure) for fulfillment, with those that don't conform being shoved out. All kinds of fine-tuning has been done to make a more motivating environment, and most of it is good. Yet, it still falls short, as I watch a continual turnover of salespeople I would call really capable people. In more recent years, I have watched as scientific personality tests have been used to determine the *fitness* of a salesperson candidate (also good, but still falling short). All of these strategies fall short because they fail to address the individuals' belief systems and the subconscious "rules" that they have set for themselves.

To motivate salespeople in a permanent fashion, it is first necessary to discover what is important to them. What makes you happy? What does success mean to you? What makes you feel fulfilled in life? Open-ended questions like these will help you and the salesperson understand what brings him or her pleasure. Humans will subconsciously, through their belief systems, do whatever they need to do to bring themselves that pleasure.

When people first get their real estate license, they are brimming with excitement! Oh, the possibilities! The freedom! The personal fulfillment! They have envisioned the future, and they are motivated! Then, as the manager, you give them a policy and procedure handbook, send them to MLS and Realtor orientations, show them some office tools to help them, and hope they have what it takes. If you're a really good manager, you even get them into training or mentoring. It really is sink or swim! Unless the salespeople are really self-motivated with exceptional self-awareness, they will be demotivated in a very short time. So uncovering, both for you and for your salespeople, what their belief systems are is a vital first step toward motivation. In addition to, or in lieu of the open-ended questions, you can also have them identify their priority values (á la Tony Robbins) from a list like this:

Place these values in order from which one is most important to your fulfillment and pleasure at the top, to the least important at the bottom.

Love	_____
Success	_____
Freedom	_____
Intimacy	_____
Security	_____
Adventure	_____
Power	_____
Passion	_____
Comfort	_____
Health	_____
Fun	_____
Contribution	_____
Admiration	_____
Respect	_____

After establishing what they move toward, ask them, "What has to happen in order for you to feel _____? And it is just as important to know what *pain* they avoid. Have them identify the three things that cause them the most pain out of rejection, anger, frustration, loneliness, guilt, depression, humiliation, pressure, and stress. Whatever it is they identify that brings them the most pain, their subconscious mind will find innumerable ways to avoid the activities that would bring it to them. I repeat, the first step a manager takes in motivating salespeople is to find, both for them and for the manager, what values or feelings they cherish and will gravitate toward and which feelings they will avoid.

Step 2 is to determine, together with the salespeople, which specific real estate activities will elicit which results—gravitation toward or avoidance of which emotions. As a simple explanation, if I sit on the couch doing nothing but watching television, I will get lethargic and feel guilt and depression. My mind will seek reprieve from that pain and find something that will replace that negative emotion with positive emotions, so it will conjure up a mental image of eating ice cream (and the emotions of comfort, security, and freedom that I associate with the act of eating ice cream), and I will be driven subconsciously to seek out ice cream. Recognizing the destructive pattern, I know that I must stop watching television or I will weigh three hundred pounds. The act of watching television for any prolonged period will be destructive to me.

Now here is a real estate sales example. A salesperson indicates that success is extremely important to her and success to her is defined as closing two transactions each month. She will need a good prospecting and lead-generation plan. But if the top pain for her is rejection, having a prospecting plan involving cold-calling will result in disaster. While engulfed in the pain (rejection) of cold-calling, her mind will seek reprieve and focus on something that will deliver her pleasure—often something destructive. Demotivation occurs when the salesperson feels hopelessness. It wouldn't matter if all of Maslow's hierarchy levels were met; the subconscious mind of the human being would steer her away from the pain of rejection. If her number 2 pain is stress, she is going to feel stress from the desire to succeed but a conflict with rejection avoidance. This person must be presented a prospecting and lead-generation plan that her belief systems will accept, which will not include rejection and stress and that will bring her two closings each month. She also needs to do some rules changing about what constitutes rejection and what constitutes stress, in her own mind. The real estate activities must be congruent with the person's desires for pleasure and her avoidance of pain.

Continuing with this example, let's say that she determines that she will only prospect within her existing sphere of influence, involve herself in her church, a local volleyball league, and a gourmet dinner group. Her belief system won't buy off on all that fun stuff bringing her success, so you must show her a logical plan that her conscious faculty and subconscious faculty of her mind will both accept. Draw out for her, on a piece of paper, that to work five days a week, fifty weeks a year, she will need 8,640 contacts per year. Clearly define with her what it is that constitutes a contact. According to national averages, that number of contacts should result in 144 annual appointments, and ultimately the twenty-four closed transactions that she is seeking to feel success, her number 1 priority. Between personal visits, phone calls, and e-mails with her sphere of influence, her dinner group, her volleyball league, and her church, she must make thirty-five contacts each day, five days a week. She must visualize the activities and conversations. Her subconscious mind must buy off on it!

Step 3 is that the salesperson must allow herself to be held accountable. She must understand how the subconscious mind and creative imagination work and to embrace accountability as the only way to accomplish the thirty-five contacts per day. When the salesperson understands the workings of her own mind, she will know how to reward herself daily for the thirty-five contacts and what the pain will be for having to give the accounting of not doing it. (Remember that in this example, rejection and stress are her two top pains.)

This three-step plan for motivation helps the salesperson identify what it is that gives her pleasure and what it is that gives her pain—which activities will bring pleasure and avoid pain—and holds her accountable for those activities on a daily basis. When the subconscious mind embraces the plan (which it will because it is logical and gives hope), it will solidify into a belief system for the salesperson. *That* is motivating to a salesperson. It is motivating to feel hope. It is motivating for people to know that they are moving toward their pleasures and away from their pain. And accountability is the glue that holds it all together.

5

Guevon!
(Hard Work)

In Jim Collins's book *Good to Great*, he tells the story of a high school cross-country team that had been the laughingstock of the league before a new coach brought in a new mind-set. His premise was that (and I paraphrase here) we run the hardest at the end, because we know that talent will vary and that at the end of the race, our opponents will be feeling as bad as we do, with aching muscles, burning lungs, and so on; knowing how bad they feel, we will be willing to push through the pain until we finish. We know that our opponents will not be willing to do that. The team went on to win state championships. It was a change in the story that the mind told that became the culture of that team.

In watching real estate agents' work habits over the past thirty plus years, it has become obvious to me that some agents show up, keep goals and commitments, and stay on task, while others wander aimlessly as their mind directs them, like a dog sniffing along the sidewalk—distracted by anything. The physical pain that a cross-country runner feels is like the emotional pain that a sales agent feels when confronted with difficulties or challenges. Those feelings of wanting to escape by making up must-do tasks like going to the dry cleaner or running out for that well-deserved coffee break, those feelings of inadequacy, or those feelings of victimhood are the same feelings that every other agent feels. Are your employees engaged in succumbing to these types of feelings, or are they the type who will internally say, "When I hurt, I will know that my competitors hurt just as bad and I will outwork them! They will give up before I do." Even more important is what you, the manager, say in your own mind. The battleground isn't the marketplace. It is instead the internal stories that are being told.

Laziness is a hard habit to break. Whether it's a physically attractive person who has been able to avoid work by using charm and beauty or a large, easily tiring person who has learned clever ways to avoid work, these people need to be identified. My wife is a native-born Spanish speaker and jokingly refers to me or to one of our children as "*guevon*" when we are being lazy around the house. It is a slightly off-color term, but it usually gets us laughing and hopping up to help out. Although laziness is something that can be corrected, it is nonetheless a hard habit to break. The *engineer* minds that have worked at my offices have been brilliant in finding reasons not to leave their office desk to go out and shake hands and meet people—clients. Their minds are so sharp that they are quickly able to justify sitting at their desk. Perhaps this is one of the reasons that Nucor Steel, instead of having one big bloated factory in Pittsburg (a big city) and hiring college graduates, went to rural, farm-type settings to place small factories where they could hire hardworking kids who were used to getting up at the crack of dawn and doing farm work. Nucor knew that "it could teach people how to make steel, but it couldn't teach them hard work." That is something that is just ingrained in certain people.

My own experience with sales staff and employees is that an individual who is witty, smart, and quick but is also low in energy will quickly adapt to his or her surroundings to manipulate other people to do his or her job for him or her. It creates a toxic environment as described in chapter 2. This is most definitely a white oleander. This person's dress, good looks, sense of humor, or wit makes him or her very attractive, and it's easy to fall into the trap. The interview process, as described in chapter 2, is where the manager must ask the right questions to uncover the white oleander.

Examining the education of employee candidates has been used for centuries to see how well they can apply themselves and follow through with a task and how intelligent they are. In actuality, a savvy manager is going to separate the intelligence from the hard work in looking over the educational accomplishments of the candidates. Ask candidates about their education: What were their struggles and challenges? What was it that came easy to them? What was difficult, and why?

The overlapping of these belief systems is obvious—a person with vendettas, as described in chapter 6, will work only to the degree that he or she deems fair, a person with blue-blood entitlements (chapter 7) will only work as he or she deems appropriate for someone of his or her class or caste, and a person with an understanding of the power of accountability (chapter 4) and discipline (chapter 8) will welcome hard work. Your beliefs will either strengthen and empower you, or they will zap your energy. A sales agent with poor self-esteem will have energy issues. In other words, he or she will be lazy. *Energy* is the key word here. This is what you're looking for in salespeople. Napoleon Hill, in his book *Think and Grow Rich*, says, "As far as science has been able to determine, the entire universe consists of but two elements—matter and energy. Through the combination of energy and matter has been created everything perceptible, from the largest star that floats in the heavens down to and including humankind." He further states that "this earth, every one of the billions of individual cells of your body and every atom of matter began as an intangible form of matter." Really drink in those statements, and then answer this question: "How could I create a successful and happy sales team utilizing sales agents who lack energy?" I think that you will have the same answer that I did: it can't happen.

Recently I listened to a radio interview of a community leader in a crime ridden community. He was asked the question of why the statistics show such a high crime rate among young men. His answer struck me as poignant. "These young men all had the same dream…to get an education, have a family, and get a good job. When they no longer believe that dream is a possibility, they look for other avenues." Isn't that how the mind works? When our belief systems no longer allow for the possibility of the previous dream, we go into inaction or at the very least, a different, less productive action. Each individual on your team must feel hope every day—hope that tomorrow will be a better day, hope that he or she has the ability to make this work, hope that this profession (whatever it might be) is going to provide consistent and good income commensurate with the effort made. It is your job, as the manager, to make that happen. Don't fall for people's masks and airs. If they cease to feel hope, they cease to function.

I professionally coached an agent who, from the very beginning, was resistant to my suggestions and angry when I tried to guide him into action. He was a very intelligent man with a likeable personality. He flowed with new ideas every day and with information and data that was terrific. He never did produce any sales for me, and when he went to a different company, he never did produce anything for that company either. In retrospect, I thought of an agent who started at the same time as he did and also coached with me. She had good results and has had an ever-growing and flourishing career. The difference between the two was that the successful agent was teachable and willing to go out and talk to people—knock on doors if she had to. The unsuccessful agent was not teachable and was unwilling to go talk to people. He wanted to analyze and overanalyze everything before he would do anything. He would have all kinds of reasons why each contacting technique wouldn't work and why it would be better if he did something else. That something else usually turned out to be more research and preparation but rarely action. His mind was conditioned toward work avoidance, through his planning and research justifications. I could feel how deep that ran in him, and his resistance to accountability was really resistance to hard work. There have been others like him I have employed over the years, and it is very frustrating trying to understand how a person who is so nice and so intelligent can fail, but the common denominator is the lack of action in the field. As I think back on each of them, I can see how very difficult it would have been for them to change. The only options were to identify his resistance to hard work and accountability from the very beginning and not hire him or to recognize it as quickly as possible and terminate that employment. The clues that I garnered early on with the man in the example here is that he was living with his parents at age forty and justified it to me immediately with a series of victim-like reasons. He would laugh and smile as he would share, but I could see past the mask he was portraying, and when I tried to get him to commit to accounting for his goals, he would resist vehemently. As managers, we sometimes don't want to see the obvious because it conflicts with our recruiting goals. But I think of the staff work hours that went into training him and equipping him for sales and the emotion and grief (of both managers and fellow agents), and I am convinced that he was an expensive hire.

My three years of coaching thirteen- and fourteen-year-old boys' basketball helped me learn quickly that natural talent can only take you so far and that the harder workers are the ones who will improve and grow the most. The heavily talented often used *that* as a justification not to work as hard. And here's why.

Malcolm Gladwell wrote in his book *Outliers*, a complete explanation of what he calls "the 10,000-hour rule." Whether it was Bill Gates obsessing over the school computer for 10,000 hours or the Beatles playing in Hamburg for 10,000 hours, we know that by immersing themselves in the field of their deepest desires, people were able to hone and discover things that they may never have done had they not been working so hard at it. When people are profoundly engaged in an activity, their mind makes adjustments to account for this emphasis. And at a certain point, windows of understanding begin to open which previously had not even existed. Hard work creates more energy; it doesn't exhaust what was there. Hard work builds self-esteem and self-confidence while the repetition creates memory in the brain and in the muscles. There really is no substitute. Trying to use talent as an escape from hard work will deprive the talented person of the growth that comes with focus and immersion. Lethargy sets in when a talented person is not challenged and held accountable.

Dianna Kokoszka and Floyd Wickman are two teachers and trainers I have admired over the years as I have managed real estate brokerages. The reason that I admire them both is that they each developed a program for putting salespeople into action. Floyd Wickman's program is called Sweathogs, and Dianna Kokoszka's program is called BOLD! Yes, they have dialogues and they have accountability systems, but the real common thread between those two programs is *action*. Each program is designed to take away excuses for inaction and put salespeople into action. As Dianna always says, "You can have reasons or you can have results, and you cannot have both." Belief systems that have been developed over a lifetime, to avoid work, will always come up with brilliant reasons not to go out and work. These two programs of accountability are really what every manager needs to implement in his or her own office—empowering the salespeople with dialogues, holding them accountable, and setting them into action. Each of those two programs eliminates anyone from the program, with no refund of money, if he or she will not comply with the accountability component, and the salespeople have to sign a contract, in advance, that allows for that termination to take place.

When you push people, they will push back. So, what is most beneficial to a manager is to select people with belief systems of hard work and accountability—people who actually want to work hard because they understand the benefits of hard work and action—and as a backup to have constant reminders of the benefits of hard work and accountability as part of your systems in the office. Those who have deep belief systems against hard work will clash with the culture. They will need to be let go, quickly. Why do you think it is that a professional sports team can go from the cellar of their division to league champion in one year, with just a change of manager? If the team is talented but full of prima donnas, the right manager can bring out their full potential, create a culture of hard work and sacrifice of selfish interests, and part ways with the ones who don't buy in to the new culture and disciplines. When I hear friends downplay a coach's role on a team laden with talent, I think that they are underestimating the skill needed for cohesiveness, culture, getting each player to reach his or her full potential, and getting that buy in from each player that is necessary for him or her to sacrifice self-interests.

In starting the building of my own real estate company, I had reached a point in the beginning where I thought that I needed to hire an assistant manager. I was exhausted and overwhelmed. I had a know-it-all brother-in-law at the time who told me that I was capable of managing those fifteen salespeople all on my own. He told me that he knew that I was capable of managing not only fifteen but fifty salespeople on my own. When I finished all of the internal dialogues about what an idiot he was and how he didn't understand my business, I started to feel empowered by the flattery that he thought I could do it alone. If you could save $30,000 a year in management fees, what would you be willing to do? "I'd walk on glass for that," he told me. I decided to gut it out and see what would happen. My mind contrived other plans and other activities after I dismissed the notion of hiring someone else to do it. I did it myself and built the office to eighty salespeople before I hired an assistant manager, which I did only because it was necessary to put together an acquisition. I was capable. I had always been capable. My own internal dialogues were telling me that I couldn't. An outside force had to convince me that I could. At the time of writing, I am the designated broker (responsible manager) for three hundred sales agents. Management duties are divided up in the firm so that I can focus on my strengths, but that, in itself, is good management—delegating away the duties that someone else can do better and focusing your energies on your strengths. I have peers in my market who ask me frequently how I am able to do it. I just shrug it off, knowing that *I am only limited by what my mind tells me*. My previous exhaustion (with fifteen salespeople) was caused by my thoughts…my stories. I would have been limited to what my mind (at that time) could conceive of. Every hire that you make will be limited by this same handicap of his or her birth. It will be up to you to find those who don't have this handicap or tell a different story that they will buy in to.

The mind creates despondency. The mind takes away hope. The mind creates laziness.

6

Comeuppance
(Fairness and Justice)

*R*eparations! *What goes around comes around! Just desserts! Payback! Vengeance is mine! You'll get your just due!* And of course (my favorite), *comeuppance.* These phrases and many more like them are common parts of speech in day-to-day living. When we feel a sense of unfairness or injustice, we quell the anger inside by reciting a phrase like any of these. It somehow makes us feel better. When I speak of belief systems permeating the farthest reaches of the subconscious mind, there are few as gripping and emotion evoking as the belief system of fairness and justice. Watch the faces of people if you cut in line at the movies. Reparations! Watch how drivers react when, instead of getting in line to enter the expressway, you pass them all in the next lane over and then try to work your way in at the front. Reparations!

I remember very well when I was a child on Sunday nights (ice cream night), Dad would buy a half gallon of ice cream for the family of seven. Five kids hovered over it to make sure that they were going to get their fair share of the frozen dessert. There was so much arguing and yelling that Dad had to get a tape measure to measure the length of the container and with a knife slice the ice cream in perfectly even segments. There was still arguing! We had to take turns choosing first, second, and so on, even with the measurements having been done. The thought of someone getting more than his or her fair share was an injustice beyond human tolerance. That was my upbringing, and it has never left me. Nothing makes me more upset than seeing or hearing an injustice, especially one that is done to me or one of my loved ones. The emotion that boils inside of me when I perceive an injustice cries out for reparations. My favorite movies are the classic Charles Bronson, Clint Eastwood "get even" movies, where the bad guy gets the bullet in the end. Those movies bring me a sense of peace and satisfaction that the universe is fair, that what goes around comes around…*comeuppance*!

In *Outliers*, Malcolm Gladwell relates the true story of a family feud in Kentucky that lasted from 1806 to 1930. It is just one account of many recorded and unrecorded feuds in the region, including the more famous Hatfield-McCoy feud.

> The patriarch of the Howard clan was Samuel Howard. He built the town courthouse and the jail. His counterpart was William Turner, who owned a tavern and two general stores. Once a storm blew down the fence to the Turner property, and a neighbor's cow wandered onto their land. William Turner's grandson, "Devil Jim," shot the cow dead. The neighbor was too terrified to press charges and fled the county. Another time, a man tried to open a competitor to the Turner's general store. The Turners had a word with him. He closed the store and moved to Indiana. These were not pleasant people.
>
> One night Wix Howard and "Little Bob" Turner—the grandsons of Samuel and William, respectively—played against each other in a game of poker. Each accused the other of cheating. They fought. The following day they met in the street, and after a flurry of gunshots, Little Bob Turner lay dead with a gunshot blast to the chest. A group of Turners went to the Howards' general store and spoke roughly to Mrs. Howard. She was insulted and told her son, Wilse Howard, and the following week he exchanged gunfire with another of Turner's grandsons, young Will Turner, on the road to Hagan, Virginia. That night one of the Turners and a friend attacked the Howard home. The two families then

clashed outside the Harlan courthouse. In the gunfire, Will Turner was shot and killed. A contingent of Howards then went to see Mrs. Turner, the mother of Will Turner and Little Bob, to ask for a truce. She declined: "You can't wipe out that blood," she said, pointing to the dirt where her son had died.

Things quickly went from bad to worse. Wilse Howard ran into "Little George" Turner near Sulphur Springs and shot him dead. The Howards ambushed three friends of the Turners—The Cawoods—killing all of them. A posse was sent out in search of the Howards. In the resulting gunfight, six more were killed or wounded. Wilse Howard heard the Turners were after him, and he and a friend rode into Harlan and attacked the Turner home. Riding back, the Howards were ambushed. In the fighting, another person died. Wilse Howard rode to Little George Turner's house and fired at him but missed and killed another man. A posse surrounded the Howard home. There was another gunfight. More dead…

"Stop that!" Will Turner's mother snapped at him when he staggered home, howling in pain after being shot in the courthouse gun battle with the Howards. "Die like a man, like your brother did!" She belonged to a world so acquainted with fatal gunshots that she had certain expectations about how they ought to be endured. Will shut his mouth, and he died.

A story like this seems almost too weird to be true, but that belief system of fairness and justice that is deeply seeded in each of us, to one degree or another, makes us seek out resolution to perceived injustices in varying ways. Sometimes it's a salesperson or independent contractor taking reams of copy paper from the office for personal use at home, justifying the theft in his or her own mind as fairness for not getting a high enough commission split or for an office fee he or she didn't agree with. Frequently, I overhear salespeople say things like, "I'll never work with that agent ever again, and if you ever do, you'd better watch your back." Real estate salespeople are notorious for believing that they have been wronged—by clients, by other agents in the MLS, by other sales agents in their own office, or by their manager. As a manager, it is important to know the extent of a sales agent's fairness and justice belief system. The overt, blatant revenge tactics can be dealt with by policy and by the rule of law. I once terminated a salesperson from my employ and the next day found human feces in my desk drawer! Coincidence? I think it was his way of setting the world right—reparations, comeuppance—to soothe his feeling of injustice at being fired. These overt types of behavior can be dealt with, but there is a more subtle type of reparations that is far more common. I call it character assassination.

Engaging in character assassination is far more common than you and I are aware of. Often, the assassin is unaware of what it is that he or she is doing. The target, or victim, is almost always unaware of the attacks. That is why I call it an assassination.

If a church or religious sect feels threatened by the fear of losing membership or of failure to convert people into its flock, it is not uncommon for those church leaders to look at their competition's beliefs and actions (past or present) that they see as flawed and then talk about those flaws with *sweet, innocent* statements that are factual in basis but are stated in the words of the assassin, which are generally exaggerated, inflammatory, out of context, emotionally charged, or all of the above. The assassin, in his or her own mind, is just stating facts. He or she feels innocent and heroic for warning people of this *little-known fact*. This practice is gossip at its worst. The individuals so engaged are driven by the subconscious faculty of their mind, usually unaware of what they are doing.

For politicians, this is done at a more conscious, premeditated level. It is also the majority of the politicians who are involved. Some politicians feel so ashamed in performing the assassination that they delegate the duty to someone commonly referred to as an "attack dog." A presidential candidate, for example, will usually choose a running mate (vice president) who will be a good attack dog, shielding the presidential candidate from the mud. These people sound credible since they are stating *facts*, but they are facts that are slanted and swayed by their own agenda, artfully omitting certain details and exaggerating others. With politicians, even though this is vicious, at least it is in the open, giving the target of the attacks a chance to defend him- or herself. Family and friend assassinations are far more brutal because they are covert, and the target is almost always unaware.

When one of my daughters was in sixth grade, she had a group of five or six neighborhood girls who were all really good friends. My daughter used to like a lot of attention, as did one of the other girls in the group. There was an unspoken competition for attention between them, so the other girl started *innocently* bringing up my daughter's faults to two of the most influential of the other girls. Before long, my daughter was ostracized from the group. It was one of the parents who discovered the character assassination and held a little meeting with the girls and their parents, because she was so appalled at the girls' nastiness. But the damage was already done, and my daughter's friendships with those girls were never the same. Don't think that adults don't engage in this same behavior, because they most certainly do. They do it in the workplace, they do it at church, and they do it in social networking. The obvious assassins are usually sniffed out, and it blows up in their face. The real danger is with the sweet-appearing, covert character assassins. I think of the early seventies hit song called "The Back Stabbers" and the line from the song that goes, "They smile in your face… all the while they want to take your place, the backstabbers."

I knew two brothers who were very competitive with each other and very close in age. They were both very friendly and personable. One of them was frequently engaged in sincere dialogue with family and friends and would almost always drop little derogatory comments about his brother's lack of character. At family gatherings, it was common for them to get into a heated argument. Following the argument, as you can imagine, the self-professed *good* brother would step up the frequency of the one-on-one chats with friends and relatives where he could drop his little incendiary comments about his brother. Being somewhat close to both of them, I found it both sad and pathetic to see someone who was so charismatic use that charisma to assassinate the character of his own brother.

If someone called him on it, which I once did, he simply smiled his warm smile, put his arms around him or her laughingly, and minimalized and rationalized his actions. I believed him and forgot about it. He was charming, and the damage was done. Even as well as I knew his brother, I began to feel questions about him and his character creep into my head. He didn't deserve that!

I am familiar with a husband and wife who never really seemed to like each other but coexisted (with independent working lives) for the sake of their children and community image. As you can imagine, the inevitable crisis occurred. The husband moved out, and they divorced. They both felt hurt, their dreams shattered. The husband's way of dealing with the trauma was to sow his wild oats (in contrast to his conservative nature) for a couple of years. The wife's way of dealing with the trauma was to play victim. She took the bits and pieces of information that she could dredge up about her husband's new life and with suppositions and exaggerations began to work the crowd of his family and friends with her innocent comments that now seemed true. The husband was unaware, thinking that his own family and friends would judge him by his nature and by their own experiences with him. It was a silent assassination of his character that resulted in seriously damaged relationships within his own family and circle of friends.

I am not advocating paranoia and suspicion among coworkers, church congregations, and families, but I have finally pieced together (in my own mind) the existence of something that I once couldn't even conceive of, let alone understand. Who could ever really know how many engage in the dreaded, brutal, cowardly, covert act of character assassination? It is, I hope, very rare, and you will, I hope, never be a target, but you should be aware of the potential for it, so that you are not inadvertently doing it or being an unwary target.

All of this retaliatory behavior, both overt and covert, is driven by the conscious and subconscious through the powerful belief system of fairness and justice. A brand-new real estate agent once came to work for me as a retired public schoolteacher. After six months of some pretty good forward progress, she came into my office to tell me she was giving up.

She explained that after calculating her initial licensing expenses, gasoline and mileage on her car, and the number of hours she had put in thus far, she decided she wasn't making enough money to make it worth her while. I was stunned, because from my perspective, she was doing well for just getting started. I calmly taught her the cycle or pattern of those initial sales and listings that would turn into referrals and future business. I explained how customer service and commission sales would multiply and compound so that her efforts would become less over time, with business increasing more. She looked at me earnestly and said, "I hope so. It doesn't seem very fair right now." She went on to be a consistent $100,000-a-year producer, laughing at the fears of her beginnings. Her early problem was simply her belief system of fairness, as she measured out each moment of effort and each expenditure versus her immediate sales and revenues. Her own belief system of fairness nearly drove her out of a long, successful career. I recognized this pattern in many sales agents who followed. They just weren't as eloquent as she was in expressing that concern, and I wasn't good at immediately picking up on the signals of that belief system. But the signals are obvious, and I should have been better prepared to address that element that exists within so many sales agents as they are getting started.

Another key element that exists within the sales agent's belief system of fairness and justice in the real estate sales field is commission splits and desk fees. As I continue to teach business management and brokerage management classes, sales agents almost unanimously echo that the classes should be renamed manager appreciation. Prior to the class, they generally have a perception that the cost of running the brokerage business is far less than it really is. And prior to the class, their understanding of the manager's responsibilities and liabilities is also grossly underestimated. When the sales agent's perception of management costs and liabilities is so underestimated, it drives the belief system of fairness in peculiar directions. How many sales agents pursue their managing broker license, thinking that that's where the big bucks and the easy road lie? It's an expensive and painful lesson to learn. I watched as a local sales agent, starting at a traditional commission-split office, left after only a few months with a bitter taste in his mouth from his misperception of the unfairness of the split. He went to a 100 percent desk-fee office for the fairness factor, as he put it to me. He wasn't going to have all of his hard-earned money taken away by the managing broker. But after another year and a half, he decided that that 100 percent office was also getting too much of his money, so he got his managing broker license and started running a one-man office, working out of his garage. It was not a good neighborhood where he lived, to say the least. I asked him to tell me why a seller would want to list a house with him. His only answer was that he would represent him or her well and that people liked him. As I explained to him that sellers want to visualize a place where buyers would be drawn, where they could visualize lots of buyers and sellers going in and out of—buying and selling, I could see that he wasn't having any of it. After less than two years and only one sale, he closed his business, having been foreclosed on. His obsession with squeezing the most out of each transaction (out of his passion for what he perceived to be fairness) gave new meaning to the phrase *cutting off one's nose to spite one's face.*

Victimhood is a product of the egoic mind that is directly tied to a person's belief system of fairness and justice. It is the response mechanism of the mind when it faces a situation that is outside of a person's control. I repeat here that the definition of insanity is trying to change something that is outside of our control—the weather, for example. And the mind will often seek out a flow of thoughts that throws us into victimhood. With victimhood comes brooding, sulking, self-destructive actions, and comeuppance—all of which are one and the same, response mechanisms of the ego to perceived injustices that are beyond our control. What are your employee candidates' conditioned responses? Remember the Michele Anderson story in chapter 1. My guess is that the Anderson family had some clues as to how Michele was conditioned to respond to her perceived injustices. Of course, they never would have suspected that the response would be so violent, but I'm sure that they saw her as a victim type who distorted realities and was prone to brooding and sulking.

What questions could you ask an employee candidate that would allow him or her to open up about how he or she is conditioned to deal with perceived injustices?

My good, lifelong friend shows me a great example every year of an individual who avoids victimhood…on his birthday. On my birthday, I typically make mental notes of who remembers my birthday and who forgets it. Those who forget it send me into victimhood as I feel sorry for myself. Spouses do this to each other on anniversaries, Christmas, and other events. But my good friend calls me up on his birthday and says, "Hi, John. Today is my birthday, and I am celebrating it by calling my friends and family and asking each one of you to tell me one way that I have been a benefit to you, in your life." I will then share with him a way in which he has blessed my life, and we say good-bye so that he can move on with his calls. This is a great lesson in life, because the ego wants to wait to be acted upon and then fall into victimhood, and from victimhood comes comeuppance or sadness. We mask our pain by either seeking revenge or feeling hurt, but both are symptoms of victimhood. And both of them hurt us in the long run. A Dianna Kokoszka quote that I love is, "You teach people how to treat you."

Once again, I'll state that the definition of insanity is trying to change realities that you have no control over. If sales agents feel wronged by something in your office, their ego will likely pull them into victimhood. Their behaviors will then become sullen and sulking, or they will seek reparations—neither of which will be good for you. The type of interview questions you can ask candidates are things like: "You mentioned earlier that you have a spouse. If your spouse leaves the front porch a mess, how will you address that with him or her?" or "You mentioned that you have three teenagers. What do you do when they say or do something that shows you lack of respect?" or "How do you teach other drivers who cut you off on the road that what they did was wrong?" These questions are asked in a nonchalant, almost whimsical way. You want them to respond without threat or fear of judgment. Watch their expressions and listen to the tone that they use. Look for signs of victimhood in their response.

"My spouse *always*..." or "What are you going to do? They're teenagers," or "Welcome to my world. It's like I have a sign that says 'pull out in front of me.'"

Victims have a tendency to measure things, and fairness is of utmost importance. Sounds reasonable. But what is fair? In the mind of the victim, it is based on his or her own egoic measuring stick. I once questioned a friend of mine's judgment when he shared with me that after work he usually returned home and washed the dishes or cleaned up the house. "But you've been working all day and she has been home with nothing to do but clean! Why are you doing her job for her? Does she do yours for you?" I said to him.

He looked confused. Then he responded while chuckling, "What does it matter? It just has to get done. What does it matter who does it?"

That was several years ago, and I remember thinking that that is a great quality to possess. Just do it. Today, that is a belief system that is hard to find in an individual, but that is absolutely the kind of worker you want on your team.

7

Blue Blood
(Arrogance and Entitlement)

Within the belief system that each person has formed is a component that I call *arrogance*. Most people spend their lives struggling to prove that they are better than others by acquiring material goods, money, titles, and position. As humans, we tend to feel that we are either better than others or we are worse and can't measure up. The reality, of course (to the logical mind), is that neither one of those ideas is true. You are no better or worse than others. We are all of equal worth with strengths and weaknesses in various areas, depending on a variety of stimuli in our lives. But the mortal ego cries out for a sense of betterment, measuring itself constantly against others. When people have been raised being told, over and over, how beautiful they are, how perfect they are, and how all the other kids and parents must be fuming with jealousy, and so on, those messages sink deep into their subconscious or adaptive unconscious mind. Combine that with that the parent's need to constantly be correcting the child and you have a very simple recipe for creating this feeling of being better than others yet frequently feeling like less (the natural comedown from the artificial high). High, then low. Elated, then depressed. It really is a mental sickness, and yet we seem to accept it as normal in our society. The defense mechanisms of the psyche (our survival instinct) seeking resolve to the internal mental conflict that rages in the subconscious mind is what creates these feelings of superiority and arrogance and also the bewildering sense of entitlement. How does a person go through life with a strong feeling that he or she shouldn't have to feel pain and difficulty or stress or that somehow anything that anyone else has that he or she doesn't have is obviously ill-gotten gain? It is akin to class envy but deeper. Entitlement also stems from an individual's belief system of fairness and justice. It goes deeper than a misguided and easily manipulated feeling of social injustice that politicians so shamelessly use. It is woven into the individual's belief system so tightly that the young child rips through birthday presents without a thought of who each present is from or what sacrifice had to be made to give it. It is the young adult who believes that he or she shouldn't have to pay for his or her own college education but that it is owed to him or her by parents and society. It is the adult who starts counting his or her parents' worth, anticipating what is to come to him or her when the parents die (even putting tags on the back and underside of items with their name on them to stake a claim—Yes, that happened!). It is the elderly person who feels that society should pay for his or her livelihood, not have a savings account or personal investment to draw on. The incongruence of the belief system with harsh reality sends people into physical and mental states of disaster where society has to bail them out, and society in America has a big conscience and a big heart, which has created a dependent society in the twenty-first century. I speak right now from my own belief system of arrogance. As I sit in a restaurant eating my small broiled fish or chicken breast and look at obese people eating a huge buffet of fatty food, it angers me to think that socialized medicine in our country will require me to pay their health care bills. Now that's arrogance! But it's my belief system. The arrogance and entitlement belief system is obviously quite intertwined with the belief systems of fairness or justice and accountability.

On a rare snowy day, when I was teaching a particular management class, I was listening to the sales agents (ranging from thirty to sixty-five years of age) talking to each other about their excitement for the snow that day. In each and every conversation, I overheard someone say, "I drive really well in the snow. It's not that hard. It's just all those idiots out there that create the mess." It struck me as funny, at the time, because that was almost word for word in every conversation, and it was amusing to me that we all think we are the master and everyone else is the idiot. How does a belief system form that allows for this type of arrogance? Imagine, if you will, a twenty-five-year-old man. He is married, and he and his wife live in a bedroom of his mother's house. Let's call him Ron. Ron works a forty-hour week at a close to minimum wage job. His wife works a part-time fast-food job. Ron arrives home (to his bedroom) each day, feeling tired and angry about his plight in life after a hard day at work. He sits in front of his elaborate Nintendo game system, playing games with his friends (who are all interconnected with his system), while talking on his elaborate cell phone to them with his hands-free ear device and mouthpiece. He eats fast food daily. Ron is edgy and angry, frequently pontificating on the injustices of his life. Now, I want you to form a second picture in your mind. Picture Pete. Pete is married also, is twenty-five years old, and has three small children. Pete married right out of high school and immediately started having children. Pete knew that the young family was his own doing, and he currently works three different jobs to support his family. He never plays video games—not because he wouldn't love to but because he knows how much money would be wasted on it and, more important, how much time would be wasted. Pete has no cell phone because the monthly cost of the service would pay for the food for one of his children. He never complains because he never feels sorry for himself. He has been saving away money for the day that he can build his own house, with an attachment, where his mother can live and be cared for. Now let's put the mental picture of Pete side by side with the mental picture of Ron. Ron's belief system, his reality, is his own unique creation. He thinks that someone or something has put him there and that injustices in the world keep him there. Pete also created his own reality through his own unique belief system. What made those two distinct belief systems is certainly exciting to explore, but for the business manager, the more relevant questions are, "Which of these two potential employees is most likely to steal from your company? Which of these two is most likely to poison the work environment of your company with negativity? Which is most likely to give resistance to accountability and give resistance to your tough, day-to-day management decisions?"

What I am hoping will be a paradigm shift in your own belief system is the fact that as you were just asked to mentally envision Ron and then Pete, you most likely saw each of them with a face, body, clothing, and voice. The stereotype that you hold within your subconscious or adaptive unconscious is part of your belief system. It is affecting the hiring decisions that you make. You see, Ron and Pete could be short or tall, slender or stocky, white or black, confident or shy, articulate or stuttering, and it has nothing to do with the deep-seated belief systems of Ron and Pete! You may be impressed with a job applicant's attire, swagger, and physical stature, but those qualities might very well be why Ron thinks it's so unfair for him to be in his circumstances. With a window looking into Ron's belief systems, an employer stands a much greater chance of making a good hiring decision. Wouldn't it be great if we could see whether or not Ron made his bed before he left his house or washed his breakfast dishes? Wouldn't it be great if we could somehow peer into Ron's mind and see what sort of blame and rationalizations are humming along in his subconscious or adaptive unconscious mind? "I always make the bed! For once, why can't that lazy Amanda do it? She never does it, and since I have an important job interview…it's about time she did it! I even had to make my own breakfast. On my job interview day! Amanda doesn't care about me. She doesn't even think about me. She only thinks of herself. Well, she can *at least* wash the dishes. I've got this important interview." *And his interview is with you!* What ridiculous stories our subconscious minds engage in to defend our own warped belief systems! It is a voice in Ron's head that repeats the story over and over again. Ron may even find someone's ear to bend later on if he misses out on the job and wants to blame Amanda. It is very likely that if you were to hire him, he would be following that same thought pattern within your organization, causing dissentions, negativity, and insubordination (not to mention a poor work ethic). Doctor Phil McGraw always says that the best predictor of future behavior is past behavior. With today's litigiousness and victim mentality being so prevalent, hiring is a big risk. (Refer back to chapter 2 for more hiring interview specifics.)

As an educator and trainer, this subject of arrogance and entitlement as a belief system hits home to me more than any other. I didn't even realize how powerful this belief system was until I recently had a real estate agent with fifteen years of productive experience in a marketing class that I taught. He was sitting in the front row (a seat usually shunned by sales agents) and was completely engulfed in the discussions. At respectful intervals, he would explore a given thought, which we had just covered, with his own insights, expressed respectfully in the form of questions. His insights were brilliant, and after class was over, I asked him about other classes that he had taken from other teachers. I found that he took every opportunity to attend classes, and he shared some of his favorite recent lessons with me. I checked the MLS records and saw that he was a successful sales agent. "Why," I asked myself, "are sales agents like this so rare? Why do so many take just the minimal requirement that they need to satisfy continuing education (CE) requirements and no more?" I believe that the perfect parallel to this quandary is the teenager.

Teenagers, generally speaking, hit a point in their early life when they think that they have it all figured out, so much so that they look at their parents as suckers who missed the boat and have nothing of note or import to share with them. I even saw a paper tacked on the refrigerator of someone's house that said, "To my teenagers: Quick, pack up and get out of the house now, while you know everything and still have all the answers!" To parents, the concept of their children growing and learning is exciting, but becomes morbidly humorous and frustrating when they believe that they know it all, while the parent knows that they have only touched the tip of the iceberg and have a whole lifetime of new experiences and learning awaiting them. This seems to be a prevalent belief system among many real estate sales agents.

When I was just getting a start as a real estate sales agent in 1984, quite often, my dad would take me to lunch. We used to go to a cafeteria-style eatery where there were some state office buildings across the street. I had been feeling pretty low one day as I was faced with the challenge of making sales and frankly feeling pretty sorry for myself. Dad and I watched as the noon whistle blew and the state employees came in droves across the street to the eatery where we sat having our lunch. My dad pointed out to me a younger man who was struggling to get across the street. He was about four feet tall and physically deformed in many ways. He was wearing a white shirt and tie with a state employee security tag hanging around his neck. Dad commented to me on how admirable it was that he could carry on employment with his obvious physical challenges. Dad seemed totally fixated on the young man as he entered the luncheon room. We watched him struggle to get a tray and select items for his lunch as he moved along in the lunch line. Suddenly his tray of food went flying to the ground, and I heard a hideous *thud*. Wham! He hit the ground very hard, having a seizure. It was all quite shocking to me, having never seen a seizure before. A couple of people tried to help, but those who were familiar with his situation moved everyone away to give him room. The seizure passed, and as he started to get up, a couple of people tried to help him clean up the spilled tray, but he shooed them away politely, insisting that he do it all himself. He then cleaned up his mess, got a new tray (with just a couple items this time), and paid for them. He seemed to be arguing with the proprietor as he paid. Straining to listen, Dad and I realized that the young man was insisting that he pay for the spilled food and did, in spite of the proprietor's resistance. Before the distraction, I had been telling my dad about a sports hero of mine and about a political hero of mine. Immediately after the incident, my dad calmly said to me, "That's my hero." My eyes opened wide as he went on, "Here is a young man with challenges in his life that I can't even begin to comprehend, and he asks nothing of anybody. In fact, he refuses anybody's help, taking complete responsibility for his own actions with no sense of self-pity or entitlement. That's my hero." Gulp! I had been on my pity pot and now this! I thought long and hard about that moment—how it was that I had all my faculties, physical normalcies, and even a dad buying me lunch—and I was feeling sorry for myself! The vision and memory of that moment has never left me, and he has been my hero ever since.

The belief system of entitlement is a by-product of the belief system of arrogance. When individuals have formed, in their subconscious mind, the "reality" that "I am a living, breathing person and am therefore entitled to have certain necessities provided for me by society," it never really occurs to them (neither on the conscious level nor on the subconscious level) that the "society" they are assuming will care for them from cradle to grave is in actuality *other people's money*, which those other people have obtained by hard work and risk, and it is now being extracted from them through taxation. I became aware recently of a young adult who felt an entitlement to a several-hundred-dollar purchase and convinced her father to buy it for her. To do that, he had to make some individual sacrifices. Within the next week, circumstances changed, and the young lady returned the purchased item to the store and got the cash from the return. It never even dawned on her that it was her father's money. In her mind, it was hers. She quickly blew through the money on other things and began asking for more money from her father for things that she somehow felt entitled to. And she is an adult! Where exactly this arrogance or entitlement stems from is a whole separate discussion. Perhaps it was when the small child just dropped clothes or toys on the floor, and his or her mom or dad would pick it up for him or her instead of teaching the child self-reliance and personal responsibility. My personal feeling is that it is totally learned behavior—all nurture and no nature in this one.

There were two individual showdowns I had, as a manager, that taught me to draw the line when an entitlement-rich blue-blood sales agent arrogantly approached me with a demand that help define this dynamic. The first was what an office manager of mine and I came to call "the pencil sharpener," as it became a symbol of everything involving this clash of belief systems. One day she came into my office and demanded that I buy an electric pencil sharpener. "We use pens in all contracts", I told her. She said, "Buy it today or I'm going to go work for the competition across town!" I went into my office manager's office to get a check for my new purchase and she told me she wouldn't give it to me. "What? I could fire you right now." "Go ahead and fire me. It's the wrong thing to do and I won't participate in it", she said. "If that agent leaves us then good riddance!" I held strong and told that sales agent that I wouldn't buy it because it didn't meet our criteria of benefiting all sales agents equally. "Okay", she said in a sing-songy tone, trying to sound menacing to me. She never left and never brought it up again. The second incident was when a sales agent had been with me for a year and then came into my office telling me that he was now going to get a 70-30 split of his commissions with the office, or else he would go to a competitor across town. I left my office having told him to wait for me, and returned with all of his termination paperwork. "You'd rather not have me than have me at 70%-30% commission split?" "No", I said, "I'd rather not have you at all than have a sales agent that thinks he's better than everyone else in the company and better than all of my systems for cash flow." This entitlement component of the arrogance belief system is so powerful that it can tip or shift the balance of power within a real estate company!

The shifting or establishment of control of a real estate office happens in an almost imperceptible way. The sales agents, with a belief system of arrogance, will expect that certain things will be provided for them at no cost. It's their entitlement! They will assume that it doesn't cost the manager of the company any money to hang their license. If the manager buys into the arrogant agent's belief system (with its subsequent culture), the control of company spending is gone. The inmates are running the institution! Some sales agents' belief system of arrogance gives them a sense of worth and ego that drives them to succeed. But experience has shown me that even those successful agents who have a belief system of arrogance will corrode the fabric of your office culture. One very high-producing sales agent (whom I had acquired from another company) approached me after about a year of being in my employ. He told me that he was going to go to a different office to work out of because, he said, "At my previous office when I came in to the office each day, other agents stared at me with awe and would do anything to get in a word with me. I was highly respected. At your office no one even looks my way when I walk in. They don't understand who I am! This new office that I'm going to...well, they all gawked at me when I walked into that manager's office. I felt respected. I want to get that back." Nice guy. High producer. Hard worker. Arrogant.

The opposite of entitlement is gratitude. A person who feels entitled to everything cannot feel gratitude. When gratitude is felt, one recognizes that one's work environment is not just a coincidence. Someone is paying for it, has nurtured it to be like it is, and has had a plan to bring it about. Casting pearls before the swine is what it feels like when you bring talented agents on board, arm them with training and tools, surround them with success models and training, and then have them grumbling about the fly in the lighting fixture. (Yes, that happened to me.) Once, at a financially low point in my life, I was meditating for several hours when suddenly I recognized that the little apartment I was living in was actually pretty large and had a brick fireplace, two full baths, hot and cold running water, instant electric heat, a deck that was hidden in the trees so that I felt like I was in a tree house, and beautiful landscaping that a gardener took care of. Solomon would have felt envious. Going through that meditation and thought process changed me. It enabled me to move forward without feeling like a victim. People who feel gratitude, and not entitlement, are usually outwardly recognizable. Their expressions show it, and their words and tone make it clear. But sometimes it masks a white oleander.

Before employing people as staff or sales agents, evaluate their level of arrogance by asking open-ended questions that will reveal their attitudes, as discussed in chapter 2. Try to discover how teachable they are and will be over a sustained period of time. Try to discover their level of sense of entitlement. An evaluation of their general feelings of gratitude for what they have and for what others have done for them is a great yardstick to use. I have found that an individual's attitude of gratitude has direct relevance to his or her feelings of entitlement. Examine your existing staff and sales agents, and terminate from your employ those who have an arrogant belief system with strong feelings of entitlement. If you don't terminate them now, they will rot the culture of your company and then they will quit anyway, taking other salespeople with them. It takes courage on your part to fire them, but it is not beneath you to do it.

It is important that you, as the manager, are aware of your own belief system of arrogance. Without being honest with yourself as to what entitlements you yourself may feel (just because you are the manager or owner), you can't replace those feelings of entitlement with grounded realities that shape the culture of your company. The term *blue blood* stems from the Spanish in their wars with the Moors. They believed that their royalty could be distinguished from the Moor's royalty because their skin was untanned and their blood was not red but blue. How arrogant! What is your desk space or workstation like in comparison to everyone else's in the office? Why? When a sales agent interrupts your busy agenda with a "got a minute," what is your demeanor as you talk with him or her? Do you allow yourself to be held accountable? Do you listen to others' suggestions with contempt or with a desire to improve? Will you take out the garbage if it's full without resentment? Will you wash a dirty window without resentment? Will you change the paper cartridge in the copier without resentment? These questions and others like them will help you do a self-evaluation of your own arrogance. You are no better or worse than anyone else. Set the tone, since you are the heart of the company, pumping blood throughout its veins. Make it red blood and not blue.

8

The Swan Dive
(Discipline)

For over 30 years now, I have been hearing speakers at seminars and classes say that "doing the same thing over and over again and expecting a different result is the definition of insanity." The room usually has a lot of heads nodding and a few chuckles. It is a belief system in modern-day business that I believe is incorrect in this sense: instead of scurrying to the newest fad in the name of something different, when things slow a bit, how about doing that "same thing" better and more often? To me, insanity would be thinking that you don't have to put in effort, discipline, and time to see the fruition of a sound strategy, as opposed to jumping from fad to fad. In an interview by the Jim Collins research team in *Good to Great*, a Wells Fargo colleague of CEO Carl Reichardt said (speaking of his simplicity of strategy and relentlessness in follow-through), "If Carl were an Olympic diver, he would not do a five-flip twisting thing. He would do the best swan dive in the world, and do it perfectly over and over again." That *insane* strategy of discipline has made Wells Fargo one of the "great companies" that has endured the deregulation of the eighties and the financial collapse of 2008. I like to think of the belief system of intense discipline to one's core as "the swan dive."

When a person has a certain world view, reality, or belief system of what is reasonable or fair, his or her subconscious mind has formed this reality over a long period of time. Various experiences, stimuli, and thoughts at the conscious level have seeped deeply into the subconscious and now cause an individual to do some pretty drastic things to "set the world right." It's easy to sit on the sidelines and cry out, "Foul!" at a perceived injustice. It's the lazy and ego-fragile person's way of dealing with problems. That's how the undisciplined person handles problems. He or she holds a grudge or "gets even" as a way of protecting his or her pride. The contrast to that undisciplined thinking is a lot harder to do. It is to seek understanding. The discipline of seeking understanding when a problem arises is to first realize that the problem is never a personal attack on you. Emotionally remove yourself from that line of thinking. Every great success story is filled with challenges and problems along the way. The successful manager (whether it's in business, at home, or wherever) learns to remove the emotion as the first step. My father (the same man who never learned to control his anger at every other driver on the road) taught me from the time I was a small child that if someone hits you with a stick, go get a stick twice as large and hit him twice as hard as he hit you. A huge shortcoming in my own life of managing my home, family, and business was that I didn't know how necessary that first step was. If a problem came my way, I often thought, "Why me?" I felt weighed down by it. I already had a heavy workload. My sense of justice, my belief system, didn't allow for this "new" problem to fairly be there. I would stonewall the problem and emotionally go deep into my cave. I would ask myself, "Can't anyone do anything for themselves?" Or I would say, "I don't deserve this. I attend church and give money and volunteer service there. Why does God allow this stuff to happen to me?" This line of thinking is undisciplined and disempowering (as Anthony Robbins puts it). It creates a supposition, based on the manager's belief system, that it actually has something to do with the manager! That line of thought association is crippling to creativity and to the general thought process.

Consider these words from Miguel Ruiz (the author of *The Four Agreements*), from his book *The Voice of Knowledge*:

The second agreement, don't take anything personally, helps you to break the many lies you agreed to believe in. When you take things personally, you react and feel hurt, and this creates emotional poison. Then you want revenge, you want to get even, and you use the word against other people. Now you know that whatever somebody projects onto you is just like Picasso saying, "This is you." You know that it's just the person's story-teller, simply telling you a story. Not taking anything personally gives you immunity to emotional poison in all your relationships. You no longer lose control and react because you are emotionally hurt. This gives you clarity, which puts you a step ahead of other people who cannot see their own stories.

The second agreement guides you in breaking hundreds of little lies until it hits the core of all the lies in your life. When this happens, the whole edifice of knowledge collapses, and you have a second chance to create another story, in your own way. The Toltec call this *losing the human form*. When you lose the human form you have the opportunity to choose what to believe according to your integrity. When you were a child, you used your attention to create the first dream of your life. You never had the opportunity to make a choice about what to believe; everything you agreed to believe was imposed upon you. Now you have an opportunity you didn't have when you were a child. You can use your attention for the second time to base your story on truth instead of on lies. The Toltec call this *the dream of the second attention*. I call it *your second story* because it's still a dream, it's still a story! But it's now your choice.

When you lose the human form, your will is free again. You recover the power of your faith, and what you can do with that faith has no limits. You can recreate your life in a big way if this is what you want…You cannot control what is happening around you, but you can control the way you tell the story. You can relate the story as a big melodrama and be sad and depressed about everything that happens to you, or you can relate the story without all the drama.

The third agreement, don't make assumptions, is a big ticket to personal freedom. What is going on when we make assumptions?

The storyteller is making up a story, we believe the story, and we fail to ask some questions that might shed some light on the truth. Most of our dreams are based on assumptions, and these assumptions create a whole world of illusion that is not true at all, but we believe it. Making assumptions and then taking them personally is the beginning of hell in this world. Humans create so many problems because we make assumptions and believe they are the truth! Almost all of our conflicts are based on this.

To be aware is to see what is truth; to see everything the way it is, not the way we want it to be to justify what we already believe. The *mastery of awareness* is the first mastery of the Toltec, and we can also call it the *mastery of the truth*. First, you need to be aware that the voice in your head is always telling you a story. You are dreaming all the time. It is true that you perceive, but the way the storyteller justifies, explains, and makes assumptions about what you perceive is not the truth; it's just a story…you need to practice awareness until you master awareness.

Or as Eckhart Tolle (*A New Earth* and *The Power of Now*) says, "To become free of the ego is not really a big job but a very small one. All you need to do is be aware of your thoughts and emotions—as they happen. This is not really a 'doing' but an alert 'seeing.' When that shift happens, which is the shift from thinking to awareness, an intelligence far greater than the ego's cleverness begins to operate in your life."

Facing and dealing with reality is one of the hardest things for humans to do. We want to live in denial and remain in our reality that we have created in our own minds. A leader has the discipline to recognize and accept reality and then to formulate a strategy to work with it or around it. Byron Katie (*Loving What Is*) explains this concept well and gives steps to master this skill.

In thinking about this, I called a close, lifelong friend of mine and said to him, "You and I are a lot alike, but a glaring difference is our ability to handle obstacles and problems that arise. I seem to emotionally focus on the injustice of the problem, but you have a way of distancing yourself from it emotionally and then seeking out answers, as if it is an exciting opportunity, rather than a problem. What or who has made you that way?"

His response was to remind me of an incident years ago. "You came to me feeling frustrated, saying that you were overburdened with problems, whining salespeople, negative cash flow, et cetera. I asked you if you would have any trouble advising a sales agent of yours who came to you with a problem, just like you yourself have now brought to me. Without hesitation, you answered that you would have no problem solving other people's problems for them…that you do it all day, every day." He went on to explain that most people's natural tendency is to take it too personally and say to themselves, "I can't." He said that no one had taught him how to manage problems, but he attended seminars on the subject and read good books on the subject until he realized that you have to make the problem into fun, that you have to see the challenge as a game or puzzle for you to solve and "get comfortable wrestling with it! Don't allow yourself to escape by going to a movie or some other escape method. Just get used to being isolated with the problem so that you can then wrestle around with it."

You can't do that if your belief system sees it as a personal affront to you! Emotionally distancing yourself from each problem and shaking your old belief system of what each problem represents to you is the first step to take for seeking understanding and answers, and it requires intense personal discipline. My early mornings are when my thoughts flow best. Most of my creative energy also flows in the morning. I've often wondered why, but now I realize that the restful sleep of the night has the effect of distancing the personal emotions from the problem. To defy the emotional association is not normal. It rubs against the grain of most of our belief systems as to what is fair and just. That is why so few people make successful managers.

The second step in effective problem solving is related to the first and just as difficult because it involves a great deal of self-awareness and self-mastery. It also involves bucking an old belief system of yours, and it naturally requires intense self-discipline. It is eliminating the neuroassociative avoidance behaviors that you have and being comfortable wrestling with the problem or obstacle that confronts you. When I was in college, I became aware of a strange pattern that I followed. I would enjoy my classes—the reading, studying, and so on. But when test time came around, the stress and anxiety of it was so intense that I found myself doubting my ability. To relieve the stress and anxiety, I would go to a movie or play a board football game with a roommate. The positive neuroassociation of enjoying the movie or football game while escaping the stress and anxiety of the moment was powerful. I fell into it every time. In running my own business, years later, I observed the vast majority of salespeople engaged in the same neuroassociative behavior. They were trained and clearly understood what they needed to do to generate leads but would instead involve themselves in nonproductive activities with subconsciously produced justifications for their neuroassociative avoidance behaviors.

Dilemmas and problems that we face are the same thing. It is painful to face the dilemma when we feel that there is no solution, so we find something that makes us feel better—that we get pain relief from. Some people smoke, abuse alcohol, seek pornography, gamble, have affairs, overeat, and so on in order to find pleasure in the middle of frustrating and painful problems with the obvious irony that they are creating bigger problems for themselves. But whether it's an innocent avoidance behavior like playing games, watching television, or escaping to a movie or more serious behaviors like I just mentioned above, a neuroassociation develops and creates a dependency and subsequently a very dangerous cycle.

Breaking or not starting an avoidance behavior begins with breaking the flow of thought that says, "I can't" or "It's impossible." Negative self-talk is common because (with all the right intentions) our parents, teachers, church leaders, and so on have planted these phrases into our subconscious minds, and they now flow instinctively when daunting problems arise. We set finite, unfortunate limitations upon ourselves when we allow those voices in our heads to go unchecked. The logical mind almost becomes an enemy when it comes to problem solving, because when the finite, negative inner-voice-influenced mind can't grab an immediate solution, it seeks reprieve from the frustration…like a monster! It (the mind) can't endure the pain, frustration, and fear of the unsolved problem. So it seeks relief through avoidance behaviors that it gets a neuroassociative pleasure from (either past or imagined). It all begins with a negative thought like, "This is an impossible dilemma," or "Why me?" These types of thoughts immediately become negative emotions. The negative emotion is what naturally makes you take it personally, preventing you from exercising step 1 (removing the emotion) and then engages you in seeking a pleasurable feeling to avoid the stress, anxiety, fear, and pain of the unsolvable problem.

I want to scream right now as I am writing this because I experienced these first two issues (without recognition of what I was doing) for so many frustrating years. I didn't create those inner voices. They were fed to me by loving, well-meaning people, and trusting them, my conscious mind accepted those negative thoughts until they became indelibly imprinted into the brain cells of my fertile subconscious mind. In order for me to keep away from the negative emotions that will follow the negative self-talk in my head, I have to proactively recognize the pattern and shock it—snap it—quickly with humor or with positive, vocalized statements about myself that will override the negative. For example, stormy weather had caused a section of my back fence to come out of the bracket that previously held it firmly in place. It just hung there with a big gap looking over into my neighbor's yard. My initial thoughts were to blame the neighbor or to blame the guy who built the fence. My rational mind quickly thought through that, and I had to eliminate either of those as possibilities, but the frustration still remained. Physically, I put my middle finger out to the fence. An inner voice said to me, "You are not a handyman and can't fix stuff like this." I felt the frustration mounting at the thought of this seemingly impossible dilemma. Then I recognized the pattern and the negative inner voices and knew that I had to break the thought pattern. With no one around to hear me, I said, out loud, "I am a smart guy. There is a solution, and I'm going to do this." The other, negative voice in my head was still strong, so I had to repeat the aforementioned affirmation about five times forcefully. I had to laugh at myself standing in my backyard talking to myself, but the negative emotion left me. I calmly looked at the bracket system and formulated a plan in my head. I let my mind wrestle a bit with the new plan and the possible hurdles. I brought out a couple of tools and nails, reattaching the segment of fence. That evening, I smiled as I sat down on the couch next to my wife and said, "I've become quite the handyman around here."

She looked at me, amused, resisting, I'm sure, the temptation to call me a dork. But I am changing the pattern of some strong inner voices and subsequently the emotions that associate with them.

Step 3 runs right in stride with steps 1 and 2. It is to enjoy wrestling with the problem. This is the step that comes easily to me, unlike the first two. I love to do crossword puzzles, Sudoku puzzles, and jumbles. I love taking on the challenge, hitting mental roadblocks, regrouping with a fresh mind later, and then conquering! It is a thrill for me. It's fun, relaxing, and interesting. Many people lack the patience to sift through all the combinations and possibilities. But it's just a game! And because it's just a game, I can relax my mind and allow the creativity and natural brilliance of the brain to do its work. It's not that I'm smarter than others, but I am patient when it's just a game. In Malcolm Gladwell's book, *Outliers*, he explains how high scorers on the TIMSS test are the same people with the patience to fill out an exhausting questionnaire.

Every four years, an international group of educators administers a comprehensive mathematics and science test to elementary students around the world…and the point of the T.I.M.S.S. is to compare the educational achievement of one country with another's.

When students sit down to take the T.I.M.S.S. exam they also have to fill out a questionnaire. It asks them all kinds of things, such as what their parents' level of education is, and what their views about math are, and what their friends are like. It's not a trivial exercise. It's about 120 questions long. In fact, it is so tedious and demanding that many students leave as many as ten or twenty questions blank.

Now here's the interesting part. As it turns out, the average number of items answered on that questionnaire varies from country to country. It is possible, in fact, to rank all the participating countries according to how many items their students answer on the questionnaire. Now, what do you think happens if you compare the questionnaire rankings with the math rankings on the T.I.M.S.S.? **They are exactly the same.** In other words, countries whose students are willing to concentrate and sit still long enough and focus on answering every single question in an endless questionnaire are the same countries whose students do the best job of solving math problems.

I don't think that there are many naturally smarter people. Most of us are in pretty much the same ball park. But those with patience learn and focus more. If we are patient in thinking through our problems, welcoming and enjoying the process, like a Sudoku puzzle, then our relaxed mind can create solutions. *Thinking outside of the box* is simply relaxing the mind so that it can conceive of ideas beyond its current framework of possibilities and limitations that your own belief system has created.

The fourth and final step in problem-solving is to implement your solution with resolve and confidence. It sounds easier than it actually is. You will usually have others second-guessing your decisions, and your inner-voices will be second-guessing your decisions. You must stand firm. If you have exercised discipline in the first three steps, then you must be strong to the finish. Once, when my sons were in Little League baseball, the umpire didn't show up. They looked for a parent to umpire, and I suppose that because I was the tallest, they asked me to do it. I did, and with my first two or three ball or strike calls, I showed hesitation as I mentally second-guessed each call. Suddenly parents started positioning themselves behind the backstop and vocally second-guessing my calls. Realizing what was happening, I stopped hesitating and instantaneously, with each pitch, yelled out, "Ball!" or "Strike!" twice as loud as I had been doing. The parents all went back to the bleachers, and even I started trusting in my reactions and snap judgments. Too much analysis causes paralysis! Follow through on your problem-solving decisions just like that!

These four steps in solving problems and the dilemmas that face you are no easy task. The seeking of answers and seeking understanding require discipline, self-awareness, and understanding, patience, and resolve. It is not for the lazy or for the person who is willing to settle for mediocrity. Most people are neither aware of this human dynamic nor of the skill needed to effectively problem solve. They prefer to sit comfortably by and just blame, with the horrific consequences. A step up from that, they will declare helplessness and fall prey to its associated feelings and subsequent behaviors. Few are willing to be true to themselves and exercise discipline in seeking understanding.

Discipline is an old-fashioned and unsexy word. Most people had a parent or mentor who tried to teach them discipline. For whatever reason, most people buck that teaching, thinking that there is an easier way, a trick of some sort, and they shed the teachings of discipline in favor of the belief system that if you are sly or slick, you can then discover the clever way to make money "like every wealthy person does." This belief system of envy and laziness leads to failure and heartache most of the time. As old-fashioned or unsexy as it may sound, discipline is the key to success in any business. Between the authors Jim Collins and Malcolm Gladwell, coupled with my own experience, I've come to believe very strongly that there is an order, a discipline to discipline in business. I would love to see every person in business make the paradigm shift to adopt this belief system:

1) Start your business with disciplined people. Don't hire Slick Willies. Look for people who have embraced a culture of discipline in their lives.

2) Have disciplined thought. Know yourself, your strengths, and your weaknesses. If you are easily distracted and easily discouraged, you will need somebody else to drive the bus, unless you can develop discipline and focus your thought processes. Disciplined thought means that you are resolute in your focus, that your business model

is awesome, that it is sustainable, and that you believe in it heart and soul (Hie to Kolob!). Nothing can sway you.

3) Be disciplined in your search for understanding. The implementation of systems in your business and the constant perfecting of those systems requires great patience and discipline to think each system through to perfection. Profit per x is a dynamic that Jim Collins discusses in his book *Good to Great*; it requires incredible discipline to discover but ultimately leads to breakthroughs. It is easy to just go with the flow and work hard. But it is necessary to be constantly seeking to understand what is driving your economic engine at all times, to be persistent in seeking understanding of all aspects of your business.

4) Take disciplined action. Staying on task may be one of the most difficult things for most people to do. The human mind has a tendency to flit about from task to task and from thought to thought. The classic multitasker is only effective if he or she can see each of the multiple tasks through to completion. Multitaskers often leave projects incomplete, being easily sidetracked. This is, again, where it would be great if you could see each potential employee's home and garage. People's personal sloppiness is a good indicator of the extent that the distraction factor plays in their lives. It also indicates the kind of personal pride that they take in getting jobs done. The employee who has the belief system of "Life is so unfair" and "I work soooo hard" rarely finishes projects. His or her mind justifies why it's time to quit and do something else. A doer is what I've heard people called who see a task that needs to be done and roll up their sleeves to happily get it done.

In chapter 2, I mentioned an office that I once acquired that had been losing $9,000 each month for years. That office had a former state government manager as its manager! I don't want to sound flippant or patronizing here, but what, or who, can be more reckless and inept at managing money than government? And that's who was minding the mint at that office. The belief systems of that office were not conducive to successful money management, to say the least, and the manager was bringing government belief systems of money management into it—a recipe for sure disaster. I want to address the subject of discipline in money management, since that is the company's most important discipline for its survival. The belief systems that people have in regard to discipline in money management are a little scary. Here are a few destructive belief systems that I have observed in government, in other companies, and in real estate professionals in general.

1.) Just a little more money will solve all my problems.
2.) Budget to determine where to spend money versus eliminating the funding of unproductive systems altogether.
3.) You have to spend money to make money.
4.) The road to financial freedom is paved with debt.
5.) If I spend, they will come (spoken in an eerie *Field of Dreams* voice).

These are just a few *truisms* in the belief systems of many people. I want to go on record stating here that these belief systems are false and will lead to the destruction of your business in the long term. Anyone who believes item number 1 needs to know that the truth is that spending will always rise to meet or exceed income for the person who embraces that tempting lie. It is a state of mind, a belief system that is hard to shake. Item number 2 is what government does, but what would never work in a business where responsibility and rational thinking prevail. You can't budget by identifying departments that are squealing for money and try to find the best way to divvy up the money between them. You must exercise discipline in eliminating unproductive departments or systems altogether and fully funding the productive ones. In advertising, for example, I used to try to be in every print medium available in my community. Finally, almost in desperation, I tracked the lead responses for a year and a half for each of those items. With that knowledge, *now* when it came to budgeting the advertising money, I cut out all of the print media that didn't get my office the responses required for the investment completely! I focused the entire advertising budget into the one medium that had the most response, because the responses were so much greater than any of the other media. It impacted my gross sales tremendously. Conventional wisdom may have been to divvy it up between several media, especially with certain sales agents demanding that their pet medium be used. As the success of the decision mounted, in an obvious way, the early dissenters were all on board. But any governing board I have ever served on was so entrenched in the old belief system of divvying up the money to fund each department equitably, that they could never get themselves to make a bold, gutsy move like that. Politicians and government don't seem to be able to do it either, as more and more taxpayer money is thrown at nonsensical projects. The other three items mentioned above are easy, fun ideas to want to jump on-board with, but if you patiently think through the merits of each of those, you will clearly see how wrong they are.

Sales agents are often very bright, with a lot of good ideas. Getting their input is good. But since it is not their money, company, or risk, they will try very hard to get you to spend money by quoting items three, four, and five above. They will even say it in a way that makes you, the manager, feel like an idiot for not *getting* it. At one time, with a very sparse and frugal office environment (but profits at an incredible high), I had a sales agent challenge me to get us a better building with nicer furnishings and so on. I told her that I was not willing to risk company dollars or accept the burden of a long-term commitment that didn't meet the budget. She responded by saying, "If you build, they will come. You have to spend money to make money." And she finished by adding, "The road to riches is paved with debt." All three in one fell swoop! I simply told her that it was a risk that I was unwilling to take and that I had too many friends in the broker-age business who said those same words when they took on big, beautiful buildings and every single one of them regretted it now. It was a common occurrence for me to overhear a sales agent refer to me as a miser, a tight-wad, and a penny-pincher. I just graciously accepted the compliments and moved on. It was always far more comforting and satisfying to know that I was financially solvent than it was to be frantically chasing the best way to delay or sidestep the crisis debt of the moment.

A very destructive belief system in a sales profession is the belief system that gross sales is the end-all. I held that belief early on in my management career, quickly getting hooked on the spirit of competition and comparing sales volume and sales numbers. I suppose that having been involved in sports throughout my life, I had become naturally competitive. In franchise organizations, it was a big deal to me where my office stood with the others in gross sales. In my community, I was always measuring market share and gross sales volume against all my competitors. I was so caught up in the gross sales that I had lost sight of the net "which giveth life." When you really think deeply about it, the gross is almost irrelevant. It is only the net sales that matter. But I was so entrenched in that belief system of the gross sales that my dad finally had to have a talk with me. He told me a lot of wise things about the importance of the net and the irrelevance of the gross, but I was so entrenched in my own belief system that I thought his wisdom to be outdated and old-fashioned. Whenever I would discuss the company financial dilemma with him, he would always say, leaning back in his chair and sighing, "In all my years of retail management and then real estate brokerage management, I have only been able to make ends meet by doing one of two things: either increase sales without increasing spending or get out the ax and start chopping away overhead expense." It pains me just to write it and hear Dad's voice in my head. He was so right, and I was so wrong. It wasn't until I changed my belief system that I was able to steer the company into profitability. That darned sexy allure of gross sales confuses our minds and ultimately derails the course of the business. Franchises and companies all give awards and recognition based on gross sales. I would love to see a franchise allotting trophies to those companies with the best net after all expenses and commissions are paid out. Since they don't and probably never will, it simply requires mental discipline to adjust one's belief system from gross to net. After all, if I was looking to buy a real estate brokerage, (or any business), I would choose the small company with the positive cash flow over the enormous company with negative cash flow every time. The ego driven always think that they can buy the enormous company and simply adjust the spending to make it run in the black. But they don't realize that there is a culture that has developed in the company or office and that they probably "bought" those salespeople and that sales volume by overspending. To change the policy would rock the world of everyone in the organization. After all, they were brought on board under the false and misleading gross belief system, and they are not going to go easily into a net belief system.

There is a broker/owner/manager of a real estate brokerage in a small community who has dominated his county for more than thirty years. I privately asked him his secret, expecting to hear about his recruiting, advertising, or some other notion that deals with the gross sales, but he simply said (with his quiet, humble voice), "I always have a weekly budget meeting with my staff of three to make sure that we aren't spending more than we're bringing in." No fads, no gimmicks, no special charisma, just good old-fashioned discipline.

Intriguing, to me, is the story of Fannie Mae. The FNMA (Federal National Mortgage Association) is nicknamed Fannie Mae. The company deals in mortgage interest risk. They buy and sell mortgages on the secondary market, under a government charter. In Jim Collins's book *Good to Great*, Fannie Mae was selected as one of eleven great companies, out of almost 1,500 companies—the crème de la crème. Collins says,

> When David Maxwell became CEO of Fannie Mae in 1981, the company was losing $1 million every single business day…Almost no one gave it high odds for success, much less for greatness. Fannie Mae had $56 billion of loans that were losing money. It received about 9 percent interest on its mortgage portfolio but had to pay up to 15 percent on the debt it issued…
>
> But that's not the way David Maxwell and his newly assembled team viewed the situation. They never wavered in their faith, consistently emphasizing in their interviews with us that they never had the goal to merely survive but to prevail in the end as a great

company…Maxwell and his team set out to create a new business model that would depend much less on interest rates…Over the next nine years, Maxwell transformed Fannie Mae into a high-performance culture that rivaled the best Wall Street firms, earning $4 million every business day and beating the general stock market 3.8 to 1. Maxwell retired while still at the top of his game, feeling that the company would be ill served if he stayed on too long… Maxwell's retirement package, which had grown to be worth $20 million based on Fannie Mae's spectacular performance, became a point of controversy in congress. Maxwell responded by writing a letter to his successor, in which he expressed concern that the controversy would trigger an adverse reaction in Washington that could jeopardize the future of the company. He then instructed Johnson not to pay him the remaining balance—$5.5 million—and asked that the entire amount be contributed to the Fannie Mae foundation for low-income housing.

Discipline was certainly the order of the day at Fannie Mae. Tough new conforming underwriting standards were adhered to, and if they weren't met, Fannie Mae wouldn't buy the loan. For over fifteen straight years, discipline drove the culture of Fannie Mae. Its profits soared. But then, in the housing boom of the early twenty-first century, Fannie Mae drifted from its disciplined roots established by David Maxwell. No-doc loans? Stated income? Drive-by appraisals? Where did the discipline go? Like a dog returning to its vomit, Fannie Mae went back to its old ways and in 2009 had to be bailed out from total collapse by government intervention and our tax dollars! It seems that Fannie Mae abandoned its swan dive for the five-flip twisting thing and belly flopped.

9

Who Killed the Bear?
(Success)

Many years ago, as I began working as an independent contractor/ self-employed salesman, I was visiting my best friend's office and he showed me a framed picture on his wall of a mountain scene highlighting a rough-looking mountain man standing over a dead bear and holding a rifle in his hands. There was an approaching mountain man with an excited look on his face and the caption, "Who killed the bear?" We both laughed at it because of the stupidity of the question after the obvious struggle the first man had gone through to slay the attacking bear. After defining what success is to you and then achieving it, there are those who will actually question that success.

The belief system that people have formed in their minds in regard to success in business varies from one of sheer luck to one of hard work and smarts. Malcolm Gladwell, in his 2008 book *Outliers*, examines this subject and how it really depends upon each individual case. Bill Gates, for example, happened to be born at just the right time and live in just the right place and circumstances that some would say "luck." Yet if it hadn't been for his obsession with computers and also his hard work and smarts, that "luck" never would have happened. In *Outliers*, Gladwell makes several good points about success, but two of his points were stunning to me because they broke with my lifelong belief system of success and because they make sense in such a basic way. The first point was how important it is to put the time (the 10,000-hour rule) into your endeavor. It is huge, because while the brain is focused on your particular obsession, it's going to start noticing everything and everyone around you that can help achieve your aim. The 10,000 hours of focus seems to have a refining and perfecting quality that the creative imagination of the brain needs in order to create solutions. The Beatles and Bill Gates are each an example, given by Gladwell, of talent that put in 10,000 hours of grueling focus in a field of expertise before breakthrough and stardom. (This is discussed in more detail in chapter 5.) The list of achievers parallels the 10,000-hour rule pretty closely. Hard work! It's nothing new but strikes many as old-fashioned and simplistic. Many reject it with an echoing voice in their head that says, "Work smarter, not harder," as a rationalization for being lazy and not putting in the time that is so essential to the creative mind. A highly disciplined work ethic is quite possibly the number 1 quality that an employer should be looking for in a potential employee—more than skills and social polish. As discussed in chapter 5, one of Jim Collins's eleven *great* companies was Nucor Steel. Instead of the traditional way of placing the steel plant in a big industrial city, bringing in talent and spoiling them, Nucor placed their plants in farming towns under the premise that "you can teach farmers how to make steel, but you can't teach a farmer work ethic to people who don't have it in the first place." Nucor has dominated their field.

The second point made by Gladwell that was a shock to my lifelong belief system was that there is a correlation between having patience to seek answers and be thorough and "smarts." In chapter 4, I mentioned the math and science test called TIMSS. Those students from different countries were given the test along with an exhausting questionnaire about their background and upbringing. There was an exact correlation between the students who were too undisciplined to fill out the questionnaire and bombed on the exam and those who thoroughly completed the questionnaire and aced the exam. An employer traditionally has been attracted to potential employees because of their impetuousness and quickness in completing a task, no matter how sloppy. The employer who is willing to change his or her belief system to hire candidates who are patient and careful about their tasks may find more satisfaction with those candidates. A hard worker who is persistent and patient—Wow! I wonder why that never before registered in my mind as something I would want in an employee or sales agent? I had a belief system that was shocked into changing after I read *Outliers*. The belief system of many employers is the opposite of the hardworking, persistent, and patient individual. Most will look for the quick-witted, fast-talking, loud, sly, cunning, and talented candidate. What would the hardworking, disciplined employee or sales agent do if a problem arose versus an impatient, fast-talking, short-cut-taking worker? Which would you rather have implementing the systems of your particular company? Which would you rather have polishing and perfecting those systems? It is possible, if not probable, that the slick employee learned to impress (buffalo) people to get what he or she wanted or took shortcuts in getting by and slyly found ways to avoid the hard work that gives understanding into ultimately completing tasks more thoroughly.

I mentioned earlier in this book (chapter 2) that my worst hire ended up costing a lot of wasted time, energy, reputation, depleted culture, and money. I saved the story of my best hire for this chapter and this moment. Edna, as I'll call her, had worked as a checker in a grocery store and lived in a distant rural community. It took me years to learn that she was married to a mentally ill man who contributed nothing to the household income and that she was also caring for his dying mother, waiting on her hand and foot. I said that it took me years, because she never complained to anyone about her situation. Physically, Edna was as plain as they come. She was not pretty; she wore old, mismatched clothes, and her speech was that of a country girl with little education. The first time I met her, she told me that she was going to take the state exam for real estate and join my office. She was as sweet and simple as they come. Yet when she spoke, she had excitement in her voice and the energy exuded from her. "We'll see," I told her. "First things first. You'll have to pass that state exam." Privately, I thought that she didn't stand much of a chance for success, but because of her positive energy, I thought that…well…you never know. So, when she finally passed her exam, she was in the office every day before anyone else arrived.

She was shadowing other agents, constantly asking questions, and attending all training that was offered. She excitedly followed up on all leads, and people wanted to work with her because she was so honest and pure. There were no false pretenses, no gimmicks, and no slick dialogues. She spoke from her heart. She was in the office more than any other agent, and she was out on appointments at all other times. Somehow she managed to take care of the home responsibilities I mentioned earlier. Edna made around $100,000 that first year and about that same amount each year that she was with me (which was about eight years). She was always cheerful and always exuded that excitement in her voice and in her eyes. If I could make a mold of her to mass-produce agents, that would be it. I almost didn't hire her. I had to really think a lot about it. I think that the only person who thought she would be such a success was Edna. Edna knew she could do it—not because of entitlements that she felt, but because she knew that she was a hard worker and would do whatever it took to be a successful real estate agent. From the beginning, she saw herself as successful even though I couldn't see it.

When I initially interviewed her, I asked the right question, but I didn't listen to her. I asked her how she saw herself in a year and in five years doing real estate sales. She smiled and said, "You know, I see myself driving a nice car that I don't have to be constantly fixing, making lots of friends, helping lots of people, including my family, and being a top producer." She had excitement in her voice and spoke deliberately. I didn't pay attention. I only thought of how simple she looked. *How the employee candidates see themselves is far more important than how you see them.* If they see themselves as successful because of hard work and good values, that is a recipe for success. An individual with entitlements or who is a "blue blood" and thinks success will be delivered to him or her will almost always fail. An individual who believes that others' success has more to do with luck than anything else is also destined to fail, as he or she will be self-made victims throughout his or her attempts to succeed.

"You didn't build that!" That statement by Barack Obama caused many businesspeople to cringe and cry, "Of course I built this!" What President

Obama was saying is that we can utilize our environs to create the business but must recognize that something else created the environment. Others created the wisdom in you to recognize opportunity. Those who achieve success in their business recognize that. But there are people with a belief system that sees the success of others as a personal attack on them. They will try to discredit the successful or at the very least downplay the success. They, deep down, hate seeing others achieve success. "No fair!" as my children used to scream at each other. What is the attitude toward success that the salesperson candidate has? Say, "So-and-so is working in this community and making good money and achieving success. What do you think of her?"

Then just patiently listen for clues as to how your candidates view success. Their belief system of success will have a large bearing on their performance as your employee.

10

Of Machiavelli And Iron
(Conclusion)

Niccolo Machiavelli, born in Florence, Italy, in 1469 was an Italian Renaissance diplomat and writer. Machiavellian thought has long been discussed and debated, for good and (more recently) for bad. I want to make it clear here that I am differentiating between Machiavelli's principles and the villainized Machiavellian aberration used to demonize political opponents in modern times. Machiavelli believed that people are inherently evil by nature, that they are selfish and self-interested. The *evil* part is frequently debated by philosophers and psychologists, but that is not the concern here. The selfish and self-interested part is highly relevant.

In the Machiavellian (not the distorted Machiavellian aberration) style of management, maintaining respect and control in the office (while eliciting admiration and love from the staff and salespeople) is the ideal leadership style for cultivating a culture of discipline and accountability; it is also important to understand that you are not a boss, not a tyrant, not an employee of the salespeople, and not an enabler. Indeed, you *are* in an unusual position as the manager of independent contractors. You are not responsible to withhold and pay their federal taxes for them, but you are responsible to pay federal unemployment taxes for them, and in many states (like Washington), you pay a monthly Labor and Industries tax for them. You bear the burden of the overhead of the company with the hope that you will be able to manage things in such a way that you can pay that overhead and still make a profit for the company. (The independent contractors and staff do not share that responsibility with you.) Those sales agents are daily free agents who are able to go to any brokerage firm at any time. It really is quite a quandary! The Machiavellian style (not the Machiavellian aberration) is important to implement with this caveat: neither boss, employee, servant, nor tyrant, your role is to be like *iron*.

In the 2006 business book *The Starfish and the Spider*, it is explained that if you "take nitrogen and hydrogen, two of the most common elements on earth, put them in a container, close the lid, come back a day later…nothing will have happened. But add ordinary iron to the equation and you'll get ammonia, an important ingredient in fertilizers, polymers, and glass cleaners. The thing is, ammonia doesn't have any iron in it—it's made solely of hydrogen and nitrogen. The iron in the equation remains unchanged: it just facilitates the bonding of hydrogen and nitrogen in a certain way. **Iron is a catalyst**. In chemistry, a catalyst is any element or compound that initiates a reaction without fusing into that reaction."

The management style of a nurturer risks being an enabler and creating a sick environment. The management style of the tyrant risks resentment and mutiny. The management style of iron is leading by example and implementing systems "to initiate a reaction without fusing into that reaction." A catalyst!

Accepting responsibility for the emotional and mental health of the firm's culture is unavoidable. Taking the stand that "these sales agents are independent contractors and are responsible for their own success or failure, so I'm going to sit in my little office here and field questions and put out fires" is certain doom—but preceded by intense pain. If these sales agents weren't strong-willed people, they wouldn't be doing real estate sales. They have strong wills and strong belief systems. Like the Machiavellian "prince," your task is to understand these belief systems and establish healthy business systems that will act as iron with hydrogen and nitrogen—*a catalyst*—that will bring out the best in each individual. You are not to infuse yourself into the reaction but rather to administer the right elements (systems) that will be necessary to create your desired office culture. The right systems will give sales agents structure in an otherwise (seemingly) unstable environment. The right systems will hold each sales agent accountable (discussed in chapter 4) as an automaton, sustaining internal motivation and balance on the "firm←------→sales agent continuum (discussed in chapter 3). In classic Machiavellian style, you keep the possibilities of secret meetings and mutinies from happening by eliminating both the physical venues inside the office and the white oleanders and prima donnas (discussed in chapter 2). Apply rigid discipline in keeping spending lower than income and also in your thoughts and problem solving. Stay on task every day with an enjoyment of working hard so that your example sets the tone. And the right recruiting and selection systems will give you the right people to embrace and fulfill your firm's goals. Do not expect immediate transformations in your company. Instead, expect obstacles and hurdles as people's basic human nature and wrong belief systems fight against your (Machiavellian) attempts to cultivate a culture of discipline and accountability. Don't waver! Be resolute in your course and be resolute in your business model. Remember that energy applied to matter creates all things. It has created planets, galaxies, you, and me; it can certainly create an office culture that will sustain your firm in a state of profitability. In classic Machiavellian style, you apply "push and pull" pressures through your company's systems, drawing respect, admiration, and love from the sales agents in your employ; those with sick belief systems will fear you because they know that you will not change for them. They know that *they* must change *their* belief systems to conform to yours or find another Kolob (chapter 3). You *know* that you will succeed, for that is within your belief system of success, and the sales agent community knows that to have that success, they must assimilate those belief systems or "no admittance" into your firm.

In Warren Bennis's book *On Becoming a Leader*, he addresses the following issues that form a person by giving one hope of changing those old patterns through choice and reinventing oneself. He offers the following to identify the root of who you are.

Psychoanalyst Erik Erickson divides life into eight stages:

1) infancy: basic trust versus mistrust
2) early childhood: autonomy versus shame and doubt
3) play age: initiative versus guilt
4) school age: industry versus inferiority
5) adolescence: identity versus identity confusion
6) young adulthood: intimacy versus isolation
7) adulthood: activity versus stagnation
8) old age: integrity versus despair

How we resolve the eight crises determines who we will be…

1) hope or withdrawal
2) will or compulsion
3) purpose or inhibition
4) competence or inertia
5) fidelity or repudiation
6) love or exclusivity
7) care or rejectivity
8) wisdom or disdain

Bennis explains that by examining yourself, you can begin to take action to change the long-held patterns that were invented for you by your family, friends, teachers, and so on. Understand this William James quote: "Genius…means little more than the faculty of perceiving in an unhabitual way." Bennis says, "Every great inventor or scientist has had to unlearn conventional wisdom in order to proceed with his work. For example, conventional wisdom said, 'If God had meant for man to fly, he would have given him wings.' But the Wright Brothers disagreed and built a plane."

As I have mentioned earlier in this book, Anthony Robbins calls these images that are imposed upon us "the handicaps of our birth." Don Miguel Ruiz calls them "the dream of the world" and encourages us to dream our own dream and create our own reality. A true leader has to go through that metamorphosis in his or her life through hard knocks experiences. To be a leader, it is necessary to accept that shortcomings exist, to be fully aware of them, and then to have the courage to make changes in our individual thought patterns and habits to allow for the changes.

In other words, Machiavelli was probably right to believe that people are inherently evil, if evil is defined as self-interested. To break free from the shell of self-interest and care more about others is truly abnormal. Mother Teresa was a good example of that, but it is such a rare quality to find in a human being. Trying to change people's basic nature is an insane venture, like trying to change the weather. Therefore, remaining within the realm of what you can control, you can create systems of success that will attract sales agents that fit into those norms that you establish. Hie to Kolob! The arrows of criticism bounce off of you. You care about the success of each of your sales agents, but those who won't plug in to your systems will either not join you or leave you, and you must be resolute and not feel hurt by it. It's hard to love and get your heart broken, isn't it? Get over it! It's not about you! Each individual makes his or her choices in life and must be left to deal with the consequences. You must be like Machiavelli and iron. If you, as the manager, have the propensity to need to bond instead of be a catalyst, your pain and suffering will either drive you to become an enabler or it will drive you out of your own business. Be resolute.

Be resolute in your business model. Be resolute in your systems. Be resolute in your hiring-selection process. Be resolute with discipline in spending. Be resolute amid criticism and turmoil. Like Machiavelli suggested, love those in your kingdom and be quick to terminate (from your employ) those who won't plug in. Like iron, be a catalyst for success without bonding to your sales agents. Mighty eagles do not fly in flocks. They soar majestically alone. Ultimately, your sales team is your creation, the result of a healthy culture from the healthy management of human behavior.

Bibliography

A New Earth by Eckhart Tolle (Penguin Group 2005)

Awaken The Giant Within by Anthony Robbins (Summit Books 1991)

Blink by Malcolm Gladwell (Hachette Book Group 2005)

Good To Great by Jim Collins (William Collins 2001)

It's Your Ship by D. Michael Abrashoff (Warner Books 2002)

Loving What Is by Byron Katie (Crown 2002)

Made To Stick by Chip Heath and Dan Heath (Random House 2007)

On Becoming a Leader by Warren Bennis (Perseus 2003)

Outliers by Malcolm Gladwell (Hachette Book Group 2008)

Sway by Ori Brafman and Rom Brafman (Doubleday 2008)

Talent Is Overrated by Geoff Colvin (Penguin Group 2008)

The Four Agreements by Don Miguel Ruiz (Amber Allen 1997)

The One Thing by Gary Keller (Bard Press 2012)

The Seattle Times

The Starbucks Experience by Joseph A. Michelli (McGraw-Hill 2007)

The Starfish And The Spider by Ori Brafman and Rod Beckstrom (Penguin 2006)

The Tipping Point byMalcolm Gladwell (Hachette Book Group 2000)

The Power Of Now by Eckhart Tolle (Namaste 1999)

The Power Of Your Subconscious Mind by Joseph Murphy (Prentice Hall 1963)

The Voice Of Knowledge by Don Miguel Ruiz (Amber Allen 2004)

Think And Grow Rich by Napoleon Hill (Penguin group 1937)

About The Author

John M. Hanson received his degree from Brigham Young University. He has twenty-five years of experience as a licensed real estate educator and thirty years of experience as sales team manager. In one position, he went from a team of four salespeople with $300,000 in annual commissions to over one hundred salespeople and over $5 million in annual commissions. He currently manages three hundred salespeople.

Proof

Made in the USA
Charleston, SC
12 October 2016